THE REPORT RE

For a complete list of Management Books 2000 titles,
visit our web-site on http://www.mb2000.com

THE REPORT REPORT

Alasdair Drysdale

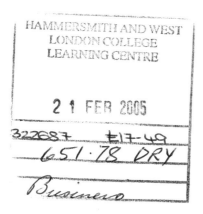
First published in 2004 by Management Books 2000 Ltd
Forge House, Limes Road
Kemble, Cirencester
Gloucestershire, GL7 6AD, UK
Tel: 0044 (0) 1285 771441
Fax: 0044 (0) 1285 771055
E-mail: mb2000@btconnect.com
Web: www.mb2000.com

Printed and bound in Great Britain by Digital Books Logistics of Peterborough

British Library Cataloguing in Publication Data is available
ISBN 1-85252-452-9

FOREWORD

When you make progress in your chosen profession you will be given increased responsibility, and that means that you will be required to write reports to account for that responsibility.

The better your reports are, the more you will impress your superiors or your clients. The more you impress them, the more responsibility (and earnings) you will receive, and the more important will be the reports you write. It's an upward spiral . . . but only if you get it right.

So if there's one skill you will need for a successful professional life, it's report writing. People who write effective reports are more likely to be noticed than people who work well, but write poor reports. Perhaps unfair, but it's true.

The Report Report, as its title suggests, is a report on reporting. It covers the content, the fact-finding, the layout, the style, the sensitivities, the logistics, the working methods and many other aspects which people seldom even think about when they sit down to write a report. Even if as a student you only need the design and layout sections, you will find it a mine of information. There is no theory in it; just hard-nosed, specific, practical advice and examples, relevant no matter what your field of reporting may be.

The Report Report can be used as you wish . . . read it from cover to cover, or use it as a quick reference. The investment will bring you a high rate of return over a long period. And if you disagree with everything it says, you will still have benefited by giving deep thought to every aspect of report-writing!

AUTHOR'S NOTE

When I first heard the term 'rôle model' I was intrigued; surely any imaginative and resourceful person shouldn't need one, but should in fact seek to be one. But after reflection, it occurred to me that anyone I have ever worked with has been a rôle model, even if it has only been by way of impressing upon me how not to do something. Many of the ideas in The Report Report are my own, but they have been aided by long exposure to the work and styles of others, and conscious or subconscious absorption or rejection of their ideas. I have also acknowledged many sensible conventions which have been instilled in me as best practice in making life easier for the report reader. I therefore dedicate this report to all the people with whom I have worked in any capacity, and especially those I have worked with on reporting projects.

I am particularly indebted to Grahame Whitehead, Colin McCulloch, Mary Drysdale, Leona Cromarty and David Fletcher for critically reviewing The Report Report and providing a wealth of valuable advice, and to James Alexander, my publisher, for his faith in the project.

Alasdair Drysdale
Jedburgh
Autumn 2004

THE REPORT REPORT

CONTENTS

At the front of each section is a detailed contents list

This section discusses what *The Report Report* seeks to achieve, and how. Every report should have a strong introduction and summary to give a powerful initial impact.

Topics are lettered - 1.1a, 1.1b, 1.1c etc.

What material do you include in your report, and how much detail should you provide? How precise does it need to be? There are a great number of factors to consider beforehand, and some simple guidelines for deciding.

In what sequence do you present the information in your report for ease of reading and understanding? How do you set out the information within the sequence? Many methods are covered, and we consider the advantages and disadvantages of each.

Style is a difficult quality to define, and it is not possible to measure. But you need to write in a style suitable to the context of your report. This section discusses the factors which affect your choice of style, and highlights many dos and don'ts.

Here we summarise many of the earlier points and consider the mechanics and logistics of getting the information down on paper, and issued to the addressees - on time, on budget. Again, there are many more matters than meet the eye.

Presenting a report orally can have a major impact - if you pay attention to the basics. And what about short routine reports? The principles are the same, but the practicalities are quite different.

A reference to help you locate topics.

The Report Report
Notes and Observations

1.1 OBJECTIVES

a Reporting objectives
b Personal objectives
c Management objectives
d Selling objectives
e Other objectives

1.2 SCOPE OF WORK

a General
b This report

1.3 EXECUTIVE SUMMARY

a Conclusions
b Recommendations

1.4 DEFINITIONS AND CONVENTIONS

a Definitions
b Conventions
c Compliance

APPENDICES

1A Some types of report
1B Example of executive summary

THE REPORT REPORT   INTRODUCTION   SECTION 1

The Report Report
Notes and Observations

To: **The Addressee(s)**
       Title
       Address

Alasdair Drysdale
Management Books 2000 Ltd
http://www.mb2000.com

September 2004

I have pleasure in presenting my report on the art and science of report-writing.

This report is designed for two main uses, for beginner and expert alike:
- to act as a comprehensive guide to all aspects of report-writing
- to provide a source of quick reference for advice and ideas on specific areas of concern

It is written as a report and not as a conventional book, so that it presents the information in a style and layout which you might expect to use when reporting. There are also many examples of how not to report, since it is often easier to understand and avoid a pitfall when you have encountered it. We should learn from our mistakes, but it is even wiser to learn from other people's, and it brings some light relief. *There are also many comments and anecdotes in italics, written in an informal style which you would be less likely to use for reporting.*

In order to cover all facets of report-writing, this report concentrates on the compilation of a substantial professional report. However, it also discusses short reports and routine reports, which, although much simpler, follow the same principles. These principles apply no matter what the subject of your report. May you enjoy reading it, and be successful in your reporting work.

Alasdair Drysdale

a) Reporting objectives   **Ref**

You should begin every report by stating its objectives and defining clearly:

- the persons for whom the report is intended
- the information it is intended to convey
- the purposes for which it should and should not be used.

Besides the obvious purpose of making the intentions of the report clear to the readers, writing the objectives helps focus the report-writer's mind more clearly.

In a very short report it is sometimes possible to state the objective in the title, especially where the report has been instructed by the addressee(s). An example is 'Report to Works Manager on Condition of Fire Extinguishers'. Routine reports which do not state their objectives often have them defined in an operating manual or a set of regulations. If not, it may be worth querying why they are being prepared, as it is not unknown for routine reports to be continued long after their purpose has passed.   App 3C

The purpose of this report is to help people who write reports in any field whatsoever (scientific, academic, legal, financial, government, military etc) to produce high-quality reports, easily and systematically. This report therefore seeks to enable the reader:

- to determine what should be included in any report   2.1-4
- to lay out and present the report for maximum impact   3.1-5
- to write the report in an appropriate style, again for maximum impact   4.1-4
- to review the report to ensure it is of a high quality before submitting it   5.1-4
- to avoid the common pitfalls which make many reports a nightmare for the writer and the readers alike

The Report Report
Notes and Observations

b) Personal objectives

Ref

Every report, especially a written one, is a testimony to the person who prepared it. If it is well presented, clearly stated and convincingly argued, the readers' impression of the writer is high. Since almost every communication is a report in some form, the quality of your communication is one of the major factors affecting your success in life. Your written reports can be working for you long after you have finished writing them.

App 1A

It follows that if you learn to marshal your facts and arguments and present them clearly and authoritatively in all situations, written or spoken, then you will:

- be regarded as authoritative in your particular field, particularly if your reports are being used externally, as in the case of many scientific, technical or commercial reports

- be in demand for more work or a higher level of work

- increase your confidence and status as a result of your ability to convey information, arguments, objectives and decisions

- improve your qualities of leadership (you may hold all the right cards, but unless you know how to play them someone else will lead the game)

- be looked to instinctively by colleagues and clients for guidance

- become more effective in meetings, disputes, correspondence and life in general

- achieve greater control over your activities and, as a result, enjoy them more

- become a better problem-solver by analysing problems using the same structured approach of defining objectives, constraints and the trail through them

- improve your examination results if you are a student - it will be easier for the examiner to recognise the points you have made and award marks for them, and if your paper reads well, he will be in a better frame of mind and thus more generous

Using the simple and systematic approach described in this report and applying some hard work, you can reach the confident and capable state described above.

c) Management objectives

Ref

You may already be an experienced and accomplished report writer. As a result of your well-developed abilities in analysing, communicating and managing situations, you are in a position in which you are receiving reports more often than writing them. Or you may be managing an investigation team working on a large-scale report, and you need to ensure a high standard and consistent approach throughout your team.

At this point, frustration may occur. Some of your subordinates and colleagues do not have your ability to break down a situation into its elements and present it in summary form so that the actions to be taken are clear and justified. What you they produce instead is a barrage of scrambled ideas. Sending your staff on a report-writing course will help, but they will still be well short of the standard you want of them. What they need is a constant source of reference, so that they can keep improving of their own accord as they work, all the time.

App 1B

That is another objective of this report. It can be referred to over the years as you deal with progressively more complex and demanding situations. You can use it to instil the standards you need across a whole team, company, group or other large organisation.

High quality reporting is as important to the recipients as is it is to the writers.

The Report Report
Notes and Observations

d) Selling objectives

Ref

You may consider that this part has no relevance to you because you are not involved in selling.

If so, you are mistaken.

Everyone who is trying to do any job effectively is involved in selling. You may not be responsible for shifting goods or services to customers, but what about your ideas? You have to sell them to your clients, your superiors, your colleagues and sometimes to your subordinates. For example:

- you need better equipment for your department, vessel, company or whatever, but you need to present a strong case before you will be given the equipment

- you can see a more cost-effective way to operate than the way your organisation presently does, but you are going to have to convince some people above you - and possibly around you and below you - that their preferred methods can be improved

- there is an opportunity (technical, military, financial - it makes no difference) which everyone around you is missing and you need to persuade others to contribute the necessary resources and influence to exploit it

SA1

Selling your ideas is vital if you want to succeed at anything, and you have to present them in a form which will catch the attention and imagination of the busy, preoccupied people who can enable you to turn them into reality. In other words, you have to report to them, orally or in writing - and you will normally have only one chance.

Skill in reporting therefore translates into skill in presenting ideas in general, and greatly increases your ability to influence people, particularly in meetings.

e) Corporate objectives

Ref

You or the organisation for which you work may already have established parameters for reporting, particularly with regard to layout and presentation.

This does not lessen the usefulness of The Report Report. Although some of the design features may differ, the basic parameters and techniques discussed in this report will still apply, no matter what conventions you are using.

Moreover, some of the features of The Report Report may provide you with ideas for improving your existing reporting conventions. Many aspects of layout and style are a matter of personal preference, but a practical reason is given in this report for each of the specific methods recommended. Therefore, even if you disagree with any point in the report, you will have considered the practicalities, and that can only be of benefit to you. Your decision on how you deal with the point will be for a specific reason, rather than for an indefinable personal preference.

Clear and effective reporting is the essence of communication. Communication is the essence of getting results in most walks of life. You just may not have thought of it that way before.

The Report Report
Notes and Observations

This is critical. If you do not state precisely what scope your reporting work has covered, and in particular what it has not covered, you may be held responsible for problems in areas which you did not cover. In extreme cases in a professional context, this could result in action against you for negligence. So ensure that you define clearly at the outset what work has been done and how.

a) General   Ref

Every report should state clearly its overall scope, and especially any limitations on its content or its quality. The scope should cover:

- who prepared the report, and their qualifications and experience if relevant
- the dates within which the work was done (very important if the circumstances underlying the report are likely to be different before or after the work is done)
- sources of information, including documents consulted and persons interviewed, and the degree of reliance you have placed on these sources   2.3c
- the depth of work undertaken (eg general discussions or detailed interviews, sample tests or 100% checks, personal investigation or reliance on others)
- a warning regarding any information which may be suspect or inadequate in any way

b) This report   Ref

This report was prepared over a period of five months entirely from the author's own experience of reporting for over 30 years in the following fields amongst others:

- engineering, construction and maintenance
- scientific exploration
- finance and business development
- criminal investigation and prosecution
- insurance and arbitration

and from the author's observations on the many hundreds of reports which he has received when working in these and other fields.

This report has also been reviewed in draft by a selection of readers ranging from those relatively new to report-writing to people at the highest professional level. Their views have been carefully considered in completing this report.   5.3h

The methods outlined in this report are entirely practical; there are no theories involved. Some of the techniques have been developed by the author, but the majority of them are well-proven methods which he has observed to be widely used by effective report-writers in all fields. The content and style of reports will necessarily vary widely, but the same overall approach can be used in almost all circumstances.

Although this report is laid out as a large formal report, a report is any communication which is intended to convey facts or opinions to specific persons, whether or not it has been instructed. Almost any factual document can be regarded as a report, and should be designed with reporting principles firmly in mind. At the end of this section are some examples of documents which are reports, even if they may not normally be regarded as such.   App 1A

In addition to the mainstream reporting topics, this report deals with many less obvious but essential matters, such as interviewing, addressee sensitivities and managing the reporting process. However, the subjects of statistics and grammar are only dealt with in generality, as these are major areas meriting a separate book each, and the report writer should have already have obtained a sufficient grasp of these subjects.   3.4
                                                                                                          4.4

The Report Report
Notes and Observations

You have stated what the objectives of your report are and what it covers; now get to the point. You may prefer to title this section 'Conclusions and Recommendations' but either way it should state what the main findings of your report are. It allows your addressees to read the overall good or bad news up front, and then to delve as deeply into the detail as they want or need to.

a) Conclusions
Ref

Every report should summarise its main findings or conclusions in the introduction. A good report is constructed as a pyramid of information, so that the addressees can approach it from the top and work downwards, the level of detail increasing on the way down through the pyramid. This enables the addressees to grasp the main factors immediately and then develop their understanding progressively. At no time should they be faced with the detail of any subject before gaining a general understanding of its context. An example of an executive summary is given at the back of this section.

App
1B

The summary of main conclusions in the introduction allows different readers of a report to use it according to their levels of interest. For example a company chairman may only read the introduction to understand its main points. The directors responsible for implementing its recommendations may read the main sections to enable them to understand how the report affects their areas of responsibility and to brief their managers on the action required. The managers and others may study the appendices and supporting documents in detail before carrying out the actions instructed by the recommendations.

The main conclusions of this report are:
- at all times, you must approach your report from the viewpoint of the addressees   2.2
- the content must be specific to the addressees' needs, knowledge and concerns   2.1-4
- your layout must be clear, naturally logical and easy to navigate   3.1-5
- your style must be authoritative and compatible with the addressees' culture   4.1
- you must plan and monitor the production, quality and delivery from the beginning   5.1-4
- the above approach is relevant and necessary to every type of report .

The sections following the introduction detail the factors leading to these conclusions.   2 - 5

b) Recommendations
Ref

Where the addressees have instructed you to make recommendations, present them, at least in summary, immediately after the conclusions. It may be tempting to place important recommendations at the very beginning, but since the recommendations flow from the conclusions it is preferable to report the conclusions first to make your reasoning clear to the addressees.

Your remit may not call for recommendations, but you may consider it appropriate or even essential to make them. In such cases they should still follow the conclusions.

If you make recommendations, state them:
- in the active mode, and in positive terms as far as practicable   4.2f
- as an instruction, i.e. 'do this' or at worst, 'consider doing this'
- in order of importance (overall priority) or urgency (the order in which they should be carried out) - if the most important items are not the most urgent ones, state the important items first and then recommend the overall sequence of action
- in summary (provide details further on if needed, but do not clutter the introduction)
- as practically as possible - conceptual recommendations are seldom convincing

The Report Report
Notes and Observations

Don't antagonise your readers by reporting in terms they don't understand; keep your language as universal as possible. Where you have to use special terms, make sure you explain them to your readers before the terms appear. They will appreciate your clarity.

a) Definitions

If any terms or abbreviations used throughout the report are likely to be unfamiliar to any of the readers, it is helpful to define them at the beginning of the report to avoid repeating explanations throughout the report. But if a term is specific to one part of the report, it is usually easier for the reader to see the definition where the term first appears.

In some fields, especially highly technical ones, obscure terms may be unavoidable, but in reporting of a more general nature you should be using simple language and should not need many definitions. This report uses the following terms throughout:

Client - the party (usually but not always an addressee) who instructed your report   2.1a

Addressees - the persons to whom the report is specifically addressed

Readers - any persons who may be expected to read the report (ie the client, the addressees, their superiors, colleagues and subordinates, and anyone else for whom it may be intended)

Field - the overall field of activity (eg medicine) to which the report relates

Subject - the subject of the report (eg immunisation) within the overall field

Sections - the main divisions of this report (eg section 3 - layout)   All

Subsections - the divisions within each section (eg 3.2 - numbering)   All

Topics - the divisions within each subsection (eg 3.2b - the rule of fives)   All

Writing - any form of putting words on paper, from handwriting to word processing

b) Conventions   Ref

If you adopt reporting conventions, you should explain them to the reader in this section. For example, this report uses the following conventions:
- people are referred to throughout as male to avoid repetition of cumbersome 'her/his' and 'she/he' phrases
- all references are to sections, subsections and topics - there are no page numbers   3.2c
- *real-life examples, preambles and incidental comments are printed in italics, and these items may be written in a more informal style than the rest of the report - they are asides for your guidance, and would not normally appear in a report*

c) Compliance   Ref

Once you have established your definitions and conventions, stick to them. Your report must be   4.2m
consistent to be coherent. (In this report there are a few deliberate exceptions, for illustration purposes only, such as the use of a different font for appendices.)

Ref (a) Definitions

Ref (b) Conventions

The Report Report
Notes and Observations

Almost any form of communication is a report. Even a casual question is a report telling someone that you want information on some subject. Here are some examples of documents which you may not previously have regarded as reports. If you apply disciplined reporting methods, you will be able to produce these or any other documents much more effectively, so that they do the job you intend of them. If you don't adopt a structured approach, expect an unnecessarily hard time.

Commercial website - a report to web surfers and potential customers on what you have to offer, how it would benefit them and how to buy it from you. The site acts as your sales brochure, but it commands a very short attention span from the buyer, so the reporting layout must be informative and rapidly accessible.

Organisation chart - a standing report (until it is updated) to the members of an organisation, explaining to them:
- what their areas of responsibility are
- where they fit into the organisation as a whole
- to whom they report.

These are usually very poorly presented, the result of both an ineffectively-structured organisation and an unfocused reporter. They may even be one of the causes of the ineffective structure.

Contractor's daily log - a report to the client on the work carried out, noting progress, resources used and any difficulties met. Sometimes such reports are never submitted; they remain as a record to support any disputes which arise over the performance of the contract. They are reports nevertheless.

Expense claim - a report to your employer or client detailing and evidencing how much you have necessarily incurred in the pursuit of his business, and indicating to what accounts it should be charged.

Invoice - a report to your customer or client on goods, services or facilities you have provided to him, and how much and when he is due to pay you in respect of them. If your invoice does not clearly tell your customer all the information he needs to know, you may have difficulty in getting paid. Before you design an invoice, ask your purchase ledger supervisor, who sees hundreds of invoices, what features make an invoice easy for the customer to check, index, record and pass for payment.

Monthly statement - a report to your customer or client showing the invoices billed to him, less payments he has made to date, leaving the balance he still owes you at the end of the month. The clearer you make this document, the sooner you are likely to receive the correct amount of money. Again, before you design a statement, ask your purchase ledger supervisor what makes a clear one.

Minutes of a meeting - a report to those who were and those who should have been at the meeting on the matters discussed, decisions made and actions assigned for implementation. It can also cover matters of record such as documents signed and/or sealed.

Staff appraisal - a report to a member of your staff telling him how he has performed over the last period, what he should do to develop his performance, and what his objectives are for the next period. It should also include a report from him on what you and your organisation need to do to help him achieve his goals.

Appointments diary - a report to yourself and possibly to your colleagues on your commitments for the period ahead. If you report in your diary intelligently, you will note in the days before your appointments the preparatory work needed for you to reach your appointments fully prepared and in control.

Letter, memorandum or e-mail - a report to your addressee(s) on almost any subject - do you take the time and trouble to make your messages clear, or do you spend more time explaining them afterwards on the telephone than you do writing them?

The Report Report
Notes and Observations

Criminal investigation report - a report to a prosecuting body on:
- the facts and / or suspicions reported to you
- your initial findings on viewing the field of the alleged crime
- the detailed tests that you made in the course of your investigation
- the detailed findings (ie evidence) that arose from the tests
- your conclusions from the findings, and any areas of doubt therein.

Contrary to popular belief, legal reports are nowadays usually written in straightforward language.

Company statutory accounts - a report to your shareholders (and the world in general) on how your limited company has performed in the past year. Given the convoluted legal format of the accounts and the length of time allowed and taken to submit them, they are amongst the least cost-effective reports on the planet. Efforts have been made to improve many aspects of statutory accounts, but at the time of writing, these efforts have been piecemeal and have not resulted in an easily readable document.

Audit report - there are many types of audit, but the audit of a limited company's accounts tends to have the most prominence. The auditors do not report that the accounts are 'correct' - that would be a virtual impossibility given that they always contain some estimated figures - but that they are 'true and fair'. This means that the accounts give a knowledgeable user a view close to the real situation.

Strategic business plan - a report to your financial backers on how you plan to apply the funds they are providing in order to obtain for them and for you a good return on the funds, and how you plan to manage the opportunities and risks in order to achieve this. It is also a report to your own team, who should be heavily involved in its preparation, on the commitments which you and your team have made.

Business budget - the numerical part of the strategic plan. Normally, plans are for three to five years and budgets for one year. The budget is in much more detail than the overall plan, and it reports to your management team the individual targets they have to meet (prices, volumes, costs, inventory levels etc) so that the business as a whole can achieve that particular year's objectives in the strategic plan.

Business management accounts - a report, usually monthly, to you and your management team on how you are faring against the targets in your budget, and on what actions you need to take to maximise favourable results and remedy adverse ones. Intelligently presented management accounts include commentary to explain the numbers. The commonest fault with such commentary is that it merely echoes the numbers (eg 'sales were 7% above budget') instead of explaining them (eg 'the favourable sales variance was caused by....). There is no statutory format for management accounts.

Valuation report - a dangerous report to write. Ultimately, the value of something is the amount that someone will pay for it, and there are usually a host of factors which can have a substantial positive or negative effect on the value, especially when valuing a property (real estate) or a business. The state of the market or other related markets, the numbers and types of buyers, political uncertainty and other factors have to be considered. For this reason the valuer has to list clearly in the report the assumptions he has made regarding these variables in arriving at his valuation. This is both to warn others of the uncertainties which exist and to protect the valuer from accusations of making an unrealistic valuation.

Invitation to tender - a report to prospective contractors on the specific nature, content and parameters of work you wish to have carried out, and on how you require the tenders to be presented.

Tender for contract - a report responding to an invitation from a prospective customer on how you propose to meet his objectives, and within what time and cost.

Contract or engagement letter - a mutual report to the parties to an agreement for the provision of goods, services or facilities, reporting to each other the commitments which have been made on all sides and (if well drafted) detailing how difficulties are to be resolved. Contracts of employment come into this category, as do treaties amongst countries.

The Report Report
Notes and Observations

Examination paper - a report to the examiner on the extent to which you have understood the subjects required of you. Answer the question, the whole question and nothing but the question. The examiner also has a reporting duty; he must report clearly to you what he is wanting - for example, if he sets the question 'What do you understand by the theory of relativity?' and you answer truthfully 'Nothing' you will have answered the question correctly. He should state 'Discuss the theory of relativity.'

Thesis or dissertation - apparently a report to your university or college on your research into a chosen subject. Really, though, it is a report to them about you: do you have the necessary perception, persistence, patience and ability to justify their conferring upon you the academic title you are seeking?

Paper in scientific journal - a report to members of your profession on your findings, theories or other involvement in a subject of interest to the profession. It may have the ulterior purpose of progressing you in the scientific world, by bringing your work to the attention of others.

Job advertisement - a report to people who have the necessary attributes that they have an opportunity to work with you in a way which will benefit them and you.

Résumé or CV (curriculum vitae) - a report to a prospective employer explaining to him how you can help him make more money. You may not have thought of it that way, but it is just another sales brochure amongst a host of them, allowing you very little space and time in which to make an impact. You may therefore have to customise your CV to the particular post you are seeking. That is good reporting practice: modifying the content and style to suit the addressee.

Name badge - a report telling other attendees of a gathering who you are, and usually whom you represent. If it is too large it is cumbersome, and if it is too small you cannot read it easily. Conference organisers generally use badges which are too small, which means that delegates do not read them, lest they have to peer embarrassingly closely at someone's lapel. The print should be at least 10mm high; better slightly cumbersome than ineffective.

Instruction manual - a report to your customer or your subordinate telling him how to install and use whatever you have sold him or entrusted to him. The supreme test of report writing, a manual should be written for someone in a faraway desert with no communications and no experience of the subject. The Report Report is an instruction manual and, given the diversity of its intended range of users, it has caused the author much more deliberation than a normal professional report for a specific type of user.

Personal diary - a personal report to your future self on what you have done with your life, and of your reactions to the things which have happened to you. It is unusual amongst reports in that it allows emotional language, which may make uncomfortable reading at a later date.

Anonymous message on your desk saying 'David phoned' - a report to you that someone called David was trying to contact you. It is a most inadequate report because:
- David is a popular name, so you do not know which David it was, nor whom to ask
- it gives no idea of what he wants, so you cannot make any preparations such as having information to hand before phoning him back (David may have declined to say what he wants, but if so, the note should have stated that)
- it does not even state whether he does want you to call back, and if so, when and where
- it does not say when he called (date and time); you may have spoken to him already since the message was left, and so waste time by phoning him again.

It would be easy to fill another ten pages by naming examples of greatly differing reports. However, the ones discussed above are enough to illustrate the great range of factors which affect what should be reported, and how it should be presented. The key is the same in all cases - consider who the readers are, and what they need or want to know. That will indicate how best to tell them.

Sections 2, 3 and 4 tell how we do that, and section 5 tells how we get the product to the addressees.

The Report Report
Notes and Observations

The following is an example of the summary in a proposal to a bank to raise finance for a new business. Remember, you have just one page in which to grab the attention of the most influential addressee.

a) Conclusions

Klymotek is a well-conceived information technology support business:

- it is headed by three directors with complementary skills and extensive track record in IT industry management, including the development and management of customer support functions;
- it has been set up to address the researched and clearly identified technology support demands of specific groups of customers in its area, and has considerable expansion potential;
- it will operate on a low fixed capital and fixed cost base, as it does not have a requirement for substantial equipment, offices or overheads, and some of these facilities are already in place;
- the directors have secured professional administration services to ensure strict financial control;
- all three directors have forsaken lucrative careers and committed themselves full-time to the venture, and have invested substantial personal capital to do so.

The directors' projections show the following results for the first three years - full details and assumptions per [quote reference to detailed section]:

All figures UK£million except employees	Year 1 Detail	Year 2 Outline	Year 3 Outline
Net sales	8.67	11.34	16.08
Profit before tax	**0.71**	**1.14**	**2.07**
Taxation	*0.22*	*0.30*	*0.72*
Working capital	2.16	2.84	4.02
Fixed assets	0.47	0.67	0.84
Net assets	**2.63**	**3.51**	**4.86**
Equity	1.24	2.08	3.43
Borrowings - see (b) below	1.39	1.43	1.43
Capital employed	**2.63**	**3.51**	**4.86**
Employees *inc directors*	***23***	***29***	***36***

In view of its low fixed cost structure, the business and the directors personally will be able to operate at a considerably lower level of turnover than that forecast. However, the directors are confident from the level of provisional orders already received that the forecast is achievable.

b) Proposal

The directors and their associates are contributing UK£0.75 million of paid-up ordinary share capital and consider that the following borrowing structure will be appropriate:

All figures UK£million	Year 1	Year 2	Year 3
Finance leases (fixed assets)	0.45	0.52	0.16
Bank overdraft (working capital)	0.94	0.91	1.27
Total borrowings per (a) above	**1.39**	**1.43**	**1.43**

The directors will be pleased to meet Maritime Bank to discuss this proposal and the provision of overdraft finance at the level indicated, with an appropriate degree of headroom.

The Report Report
Notes and Observations

THE REPORT REPORT

The Report Report
Notes and Observations

If you're thinking of skipping section 2.1, don't. You must establish your terms of engagement right from the start, or else you're in for wasted effort, and perhaps some trouble.

In an ideal world, the client would state in his remit everything you should include in your report, how accurate it should be and how much work you should do to support it. In practice this seldom happens, except in invitations to tender for contracts. In fact, it is often in the client's interests to keep things vague, so that he can demand additional content which he should have thought of in the first place. So if you don't want to be shooting at moving goalposts, it's up to you to define things from the beginning.

SUMMARY

To establish the remit clearly, you must:

	Ref
▪ meet the client to discuss the overall scope and requirements for the report	2.1 i
▪ obtain a specific remit from the client	2.1c
▪ confirm your understanding with an engagement letter, or at the very least a written acceptance of the remit	2.1c
▪ if the remit is not provided, or is inadequate, state in your engagement letter the parameters which you understand to apply	App 2B
▪ confirm all amendments as you would the original commitment	2.1e
▪ cost the exercise carefully when calculating your fee	2.1 f
▪ if you do not receive acceptance of your engagement or amendment letter, you may use a clause stating that unless you hear to the contrary by a certain date, you will proceed as described in your letter - but ensure that the client understands this	

a) Client and addressee

Ref

You may have to produce a report for a client who is not your addressee. An example would be the directors of a group holding company (the company itself, rather than the directors, would normally be your client) instructing you to review an underperforming subsidiary company and make recommendations to the subsidiary company directors (your addressees).

1.4a

This introduces potential political sensitivities, particularly if the subsidiary company directors do not want your presence, and you therefore have hostile addressees. If you are faced with such a situation, be sure to consider your client in parallel when you consider matters in this report which relate to the addressees. While you should observe all the relevant sensitivities regarding the addressees, your client will be your overriding concern. It is always your client who should provide your remit.

In such a situation, it is courteous to the addressees, and protective to you, for you to ensure that they receive a copy of the remit and your acceptance before work starts.

In some cases the client will be someone with whom you already have a well-established working relationship (for example, your boss), and with whose reporting requirements you are already familiar. In that case, you may implement the processes described in this subsection more informally, but you must still ensure that all the matters discussed here are agreed with him. There may well be features about this assignment that require this report to be dealt with different from others you have written for your client.

In general this report concentrates on the needs of the addressees, to whom your report is being delivered. However, the client is the party paying for the report, and you should therefore always remember that the client is the ultimate authority.

The Report Report
Notes and Observations

b) Objectives   Ref

The main objective of the remit (also called 'terms of engagement' and 'terms of reference') is to ensure that the client and the reporter share the same full and clear understanding of the following matters:

- the objective, content and usage of the report   1.1
- the scope of reporting and of the work underlying it   1.2
- the detail and accuracy of the content, and any tolerances in the accuracy   2.3-2.4
- the provision of facilities (working area, accommodation, access to information etc)
- the cost, timescale and any other parameters governing the reporting work   2.1f

To avoid confusion, delay and wasted effort, you must agree the remit with the client **before** you start work. If there is more than one client the remit must be agreed amongst all of them in writing, with any client responsibilities regarding the report clearly defined. The remit must be signed by the client or his representative, and you must ensure that the person(s) signing have authority to sign for all of the clients if there are several.

Once the commitment has been made, you have a duty to your client to deliver the report he requires, to an appropriate standard of care and competence.

There is the second but very important objective that the remit should define how and when you will be paid for the report if it is being produced on a commercial basis.   2.1 f

c) Commitment in writing   Ref

For avoidance of subsequent argument, the remit should be in writing.   App
                                                                                                    2A
If for any reason the client does not provide you with a written remit (that will often be the case), you must produce an engagement letter setting out your understanding of the factors listed above.   App
If you fail to do this and a dispute arises regarding the conduct of the work, you may find it   2B
difficult to defend yourself.

You must then ensure that the client sees and agrees in writing the terms of your engagement letter. If he does not do this and you still wish to go ahead with the report, you need to send him a further letter that unless you hear from him to the contrary, you will start work on the terms stated in your letter.

Provided that you can prove that the client has received both letters, you should be clear to start work. However, you may need to ascertain that the law of the country in which the work is to be carried out will support you in this should there be any dispute. You should also be certain that you wish to start work in such circumstances. You may have to make a judgment on the honesty and integrity of the client, and assure yourself that he has been distracted by other priorities and will sign the remit at the first opportunity. A difficult remit process is often the forerunner to a difficult reporting process and an indication of an uncooperative client.

In an informal situation, such as may exist with your boss, send him a memo confirming your understanding of the requirements - he will appreciate your thoroughness.

The Report Report
Notes and Observations

d) Politics

You may feel that you are not in a position to pressurise your client with regard to the remit. The client may be a major customer or a senior superior, whom you are anxious to impress to gain more work or further your reputation. That may be so, but beginning an assignment for which there are no clear objectives or parameters is likely to result in disputes and repercussions about the outcome, which will hardly impress anyone. And of course the confusion will all be your fault. After all, you are the person who is supposed to be doing the report correctly.

The way around this, as described in the previous topic, is to finish your engagement letter (or an internal memo confirming your understanding in the case of an internal report) with a phrase such as 'Unless I hear from you to the contrary by [date and time], I shall proceed as described above'. This is a well-proven route to obtaining agreement from busy clients. And be sure to copy your memo to all parties associated with the remit.

Ref

2.1c

e) Amendments

As with any contract, the terms of the remit may have to be amended after the work has been begun. This usually arises through a change in the underlying circumstances, or the discovery of factors which were unknown at the date of the remit.

Amendments can also be needed because of inadequate attention by the client to the full requirements when drafting the remit. The more senior the client, the less likely he is to specify detail - he will be used to demanding results and delegating the details to others. Trying to extract detail from such a person is likely to be fruitless and may even lead to some annoyance on his part. The solution is therefore to obtain his authority to agree the amendments with one of his subordinates.

Ensure that the amendments are agreed in writing and signed in the same way and with the same people as the original remit was agreed. If someone in the client organisation who was not involved in the original remit instructs an amendment, ensure that the originators agree the amendment.

Ref

f) Costing

If you are reporting on a professional basis, you need to agree your fee at the remit stage. Estimating the cost of preparing a report in order to set your fee level can be difficult, especially with regard to assessing the amount of work required. There are several reasons for this:

Ref

App
2B

- the quality of the information is usually beyond your control, and before quoting a fee you need to make some assessment of how easy the information will be to gather
- even if the information is readily available, it may not be in the format you need, and may need re-statement or further analysis before it can be used
- regardless of how cooperative your client and his staff are, they will have other priorities which at times will limit their ability to help you with your investigation
- no matter how carefully you plan your content, reports have a habit of turning out to be much larger than intended, as you uncover unexpected circumstances which are relevant to your subject

cont'd

The Report Report
Notes and Observations

f) Costing (continued)   Ref

Costing a report is like costing any project; you need to try to anticipate everything. The main cost elements you must consider are:

- meeting the client to agree the remit   2.1 i
- bringing together the team, equipment and any other resources
- locating, gathering and analysing the information   5.1e
- drafting the report in stages (a major report can easily take 10 to 20 drafts)
- idle time (this must be minimised by planning, but not all information arrives exactly when you need it, and your team can be underutilised sometimes)   5.2
- reviewing and proof-reading the draft report   5.3
- submitting a draft to the addressees and agreeing it with them (if appropriate)   5.4
- finalising and proof-reading the report   5.4
- printing, binding, packaging and distributing the report   5.4
- meeting the addressee and related parties to discuss the report   5.4
- making a formal presentation of the report, if instructed   5.4
- follow-up work arising from the discussions, if included in the remit
- debriefing and demobilising the team
- subsequent administration, including invoicing the client and collecting the fee
- your profit margin - it should be high, as you are providing a high quality of report.

You should also include in your costing a round-sum contingency percentage or amount to cover those unforeseen costs which occur on any project.

For each of the above cost categories you must consider:

- personnel time and cost (plus overhead allocation if they are your own staff)
- travel, meals and accommodation if there is on-site work
- office facilities, including typing, external services, materials, production and despatch.

It is readily apparent from the long list of factors above that it can be easy to underestimate by a considerable amount the cost of producing a report, and thus to incur a loss on the project. You should therefore pitch your quotation at or above the top end of your estimate. The client will be more likely to accept it if you are obviously going about your preparatory work in a professional manner, and more so if you have a track record for delivering value in your reporting… and that is what this report is all about.

Be aware that it is just as bad to overestimate your costs as it is to underestimate them, as you may price yourself out of the project.

Throughout the reporting project you should keep track of time and costs actually incurred, to ensure that you are not overrunning. If during the project there are amendments to the remit, or defaults by the client (eg not providing agreed information or assistance) you will need to advise the client immediately that this will result in an increased fee, and you must record the additional cost resulting from the defaults, and show evidence of it in order to collect the additional fee. If you do not inform the client until the end of the project, you will have difficulty in recovering any extra costs.

g) Recording of remit   Ref

It may be appropriate, if you think that there are likely to be repercussions regarding the remit,   App
to include a copy of it together with a copy of your engagement letter (prominently or as an   2A
appendix depending upon the situation) indexed and bound into the report. That makes it more   App
difficult for the client to dispute.   2B

The Report Report
Notes and Observations

h) Determination of content

Ref

The remit is most unlikely to determine the content in detail. However, the combination of the remit and your engagement letter must be sufficient to determine:

App 2A
App 2B

- the use which is to be made of the report
- the level of confidentiality and circulation of the report (ensure that the client undertakes to make his own staff aware of the confidentiality level - instances occur in which leaks come from within a client organisation and the reporter, who has kept silent, is under suspicion)
- the specific areas to be covered within the subject of the report
- any areas to be specifically excluded from the report
- the general degree of evidence needed to support your findings
- any major constraints regarding your working methods (eg on-site or off-site)
- the extent to which the client himself or the addressees are to collaborate with you, particularly in the provision of information or facilities

Beyond that, it is up to you as the reporter to make an intelligent assessment of the exact content needed to meet those criteria.

i) Making it happen

Ref

There is no substitute for meeting the client face-to-face. You will need one meeting to agree the remit in principle, and you may need a second to resolve any queries or concerns once the remit and/or engagement letter have been drafted in detail.

App 2A
App 2B

If agreeing the remit is a difficult process with potential confusion, it may be worth taking minutes of the meeting and circulating them to those concerned. However, this should not normally be required.

The matters discussed above may appear negative, but in the great majority of cases, no difficulties will arise over the remit if it is sensibly discussed and agreed. Most clients will appreciate your professionalism and attention to important detail. However, on the rare occasion when there is a dispute over what was required, you will be in a strong position to argue your case if you have your instructions clearly stated in writing.

The Report Report
Notes and Observations

Although the combination of the client's remit and your engagement letter should define the content in total terms, you still have to decide how much information to include in your report. Too much will irritate the addressees by telling them what they already know, and too little may cause your factual points and conclusions to appear unsupported, out-of-context, illogical or even misleading.

SUMMARY   Ref

Complexity and political sensitivity increases with people's status. Such matters will not be spelled out in a remit, so you will have to question the addressees carefully to determine the broadest implications of your report. Determine from the outset:

- how much they know already (this may vary from one addressee to another)   2.2b
- how much more they need to know by way of background or direct detail   2.2c
- the extent of their expectations and concerns, some of which may not be in the subject of your   2.2d
  report, but may be in related areas
- that they are fully aware of the cost and resource implications of their requirements.   2.2b

a) Objective   Ref

The purpose of this subsection is to consider the circumstances of the addressees, so that the contents of your report can be geared to their requirements.

Where the circumstances of the individual addressees vary, you will have to ensure that the content of your report covers all of their requirements. If these requirements are very different, you will need to make this clear in your numbering and headings, so that addressees are not   3.1
frustrated by spending time on topics of no concern to them.

b) Addressee knowledge   Ref

Firstly, you need to determine how much the addressees know.

In the case of clear-cut organisations this is usually straightforward. For example, a company's board of directors will have the same broad knowledge of the company's business, products and markets, but the specialisms of the marketing, research, production and financial directors will give them quite different levels of detailed knowledge. If you have to report on, say, the manufacturing process, the production director will already know all you have to say about the background, whereas the others may have to read the background section before reading your findings.

In less definably structured organisations there is seldom any alternative to asking the addressees about their individual needs for detail. But be careful, or their separate demands will add up to a considerably greater information requirement than the overall remit suggests. The general form   2.3d
of questioning should be 'How much depth do you want on...?' If their demands are excessive, remind them of the additional cost to them of catering for all their individual requirements.

If you encounter a group of addressees who give you conflicting requirements, or who do not have a definite view on them, agree the requirements with the senior addressee. You may consider it necessary to record the divergence of views.

The Report Report
Notes and Observations

c) Addressee seniority

Ref

Concerns vary with seniority.

The higher people are in an organisation, the more they are concerned with broad issues such as:
- public relations
- legal, social and political consequences
- major financial consequences, including resource issues
- their own position from a long-term political standpoint.

2.2d
2.2d
2.2d
2.2d

The lower people are in an organisation, the more they are likely to be concerned with detailed issues such as:

- technical and personnel matters
- departmental ramifications
- localised financial consequences
- their own position from a shorter-term material or career standpoint

You therefore have to interrogate the addressees in enough depth to establish the levels at which your report will be read and used. The higher the level, the more your findings and conclusions may need to tend toward the broader, more strategic issues; the lower the level, the more you are likely to have to focus on detail.

2.3d

d) Addressee expectations and concerns

Ref

It is important to understand the overall expectations and concerns of the addressees. They should have already expressed their expectations regarding your report in the remit, but what about their area of responsibility as a whole?

2.1

For example, if you have been commissioned by a city council to report on traffic conditions in the city, you may need to consider more than just traffic congestion. You may need to understand the council's concerns about related matters such as:

- the likely cost of providing an alternative transport system
- difficulties in obtaining additional land for a better road network or parking areas
- the impact of traffic arrangements and density on tourism or other industries
- environmental effects of traffic
- the ability or otherwise of shoppers to reach the city centre and therefore the consequent necessity for development of shopping centres on the edge of the city
- the social effects of transport changes on house prices, schools, local amenities and a host of other matters
- the political turbulence caused by any of the above.

In any report, you may find it appropriate to draw the addressees' attention to circumstances which, although not within the scope of the report, may be relevant in some related way. Be alert to the possibility of wider implications.

Again, there is no substitute for careful interrogation of the addressees at the remit stage. If you do not understand the full range of their concerns and expectations, your report is likely to fail to address some of them. You will then be required to expand and resubmit your report, probably at your own expense.

2.3d

The Report Report
Notes and Observations

e) Inaccessible addressees

Ref

You may encounter situations where you do not have access to the addressees, only to the client. A common example is where a business asks you to prepare a report on its behalf to support an application to its bankers for additional finance.

Clearly, you have been asked to prepare this report on the basis of your financial experience and expertise. You cannot go to the bank and ask them what they would like to see in your report; you are expected to know this as a finance professional (although you may glean some background from a courtesy meeting with the bank).

You must therefore put yourself in the addressees' (ie the bank's) shoes and ask yourself what you would want to see to be convinced that:

- the business has the management, market and products and overall capability to enable it to perform profitably and to generate cash
- it is likely to achieve the performance forecast in the report
- it will be able to meet the bank's interest and repayment terms
- there is a sufficient margin for contingencies in the plan.

In other words, would **you** provide **your own** finance to this business?

You may be writing parts of such a report as a member of a reporting team. If you do not have the ability to identify the addressees' expectations, consult your team leader.

There are other, less standard, reasons why addressees may not be accessible before the remit can be finalised. In such cases, you must obtain as much background as possible from the client regarding the addressees' concerns and expectations.

It's all about getting inside the minds of the people to whom you are going to deliver your output. It's not a new process for you; you should already be doing it in your other work activities, and you probably also do it in domestic situations, in such common activities as choosing gifts.

The Report Report
Notes and Observations

Having determined through the remit process what your client officially wants, and what the wider implications, if any, are, you have established which topics you have to cover in your report. You are now ready to consider how much detail to include in these various topics.

SUMMARY

Ref

The detail in your report should be just sufficient in quality and quantity to provide:

- adequate background to give a complete picture and to put your findings in their proper context, but without telling the addressees in detail what they already know
- proof of your facts, and support for your opinions and conclusions
- subsequent reference if required for readers working on the subject

2.3b

2.3c/e
2.3 f

As well as doing documentary research, you may need to apply some interviewing technique to obtain the detail you are seeking

2.3d

a) Objectives

Ref

The detail in your report must achieve the following objectives:
- meet the precise requirements of the remit
- give the addressees and other readers a clear understanding of your information in its full and proper context
- prove the main factual points which you make in the report
- justify the opinions and conclusions which you reach in the introduction
- provide any other detail which, although not instructed, you consider necessary to include for the sake of completeness
- provide sufficient information to support any later reference the readers may need to make after their initial reading your report (for example, they may need to perform remedial work as a result of your report, and may require detailed identification of the areas needing attention)

2.1
2.2d

2.3c
1.3a

2.3f

If you have satisfied the above objectives, there is usually no need to add any further detail. You may, however, wish to include occasional non-essential items for interest. Whether this is acceptable or not depends upon the climate of your report; in highly critical circumstances, points of casual interest are less likely to be welcome. Gratuitous information will also cost you time and money to provide.

2.1f

If you do decide to include additional detail, be sparing with it, otherwise the non-essential detail may obscure some of the essential detail, and thus frustrate the readers. If it is more than a paragraph, consider consigning it to an appendix.

3.2k

b) General understanding

Ref

How much 'general understanding' do you need to provide in your report? Understanding is not a commodity which can be measured.

The answer is easy to define, although harder to achieve. You need to provide enough background in your report so that all the key facts which you report can be understood in their complete and correct context. Otherwise, the key facts may not be understood or, worse still, they may be interpreted in a different way from that intended.

cont'd

The Report Report
Notes and Observations

b) **General understanding** (continued)   Ref

For example, the sales revenue of a business may have declined over a period. That fact on its own would be interpreted as a poor performance. But if the total market has declined by a greater percentage, and all the competing businesses have lost a greater percentage of their revenue than the business on which you are reporting, then its modest decline could be interpreted as a creditable performance in difficult circumstances. In such a situation you would have to report the result for the market as a whole to enable the reader to understand the business's performance in its true context.   3.4 i

Background relating to your subject as a whole should be presented early in the report to put everything in context, but background relating only to a particular point is better presented together with that point. It can be immediately before or immediately after the point, but the readers should not have to go looking through the report for the background to any point. Occasionally a minor degree of repetition may be needed.   1.4a

c) **Proof of factual points**   Ref

Hard evidence is always acceptable; hearsay is not. Evidence is seldom 'hard' unless it is corroborated on paper; hence the practice of taking signed statements from suspects and witnesses in criminal investigations. The process of committing someone's opinions or testimony to paper sharpens his concentration and is more likely to result in a factual statement which would not subsequently be denied. In most non-criminal interviewing situations a signed statement is not required.

Evidence generally comes from one or more of the following sources:

- interviewing people who are directly involved in the subject of the report (remember that they may have a vested interest in the findings of the report, and may therefore be biased in what they tell you)
- interviewing people who are indirectly involved through some association with the subject (they are more likely to be impartial, but you cannot be sure of that)   2.3d
- interviewing people who are not normally involved at all with the subject, but have been associated with it through some circumstance (eg witnessing an accident)   2.3d
- reviewing written material, which itself can be a direct or indirect part of the subject and its field (eg an organisation's internal records), or can be incidental (eg external research data) - remember that such material may contain errors or bias, so you need to establish how reliably it was prepared and verified, and state in your report any concerns you have regarding its correctness and impartiality
- the reporter's own calculations and distillations from the above.

In all cases when you are interviewing people, your interview is limited by:

- their understanding of the topic of your interview (in the case of a confidential report, you may even be forbidden to tell them the purpose of the interview)
- your ability to phrase the questions in a manner fully understandable by them, which may involve choosing your words more carefully than usual, especially if they are not familiar with your language or are below your level of expertise
- their ability to express themselves clearly, concisely, accurately, completely and impartially (you will be disappointed to find that this is a relatively rare combination)
- their willingness to help (this cannot be taken for granted, even when it is stated)
- their fear of giving information which they believe may disadvantage them personally.

cont'd

The Report Report
Notes and Observations

c) **Proof of factual points** (continued)   Ref

Therefore, when you are obtaining detail by interviewing people, you must:

- assess their knowledge and appreciation of the topic of the interview
- ensure that they are giving you information fully and impartially
- make notes of what they tell you and note the location, time and date of the interview (in difficult circumstances, it may be worth having them read your notes afterward and sign their approval of them if that is practicable)
- ensure at each point that they have understood your question (this is often evident from the answer) and that you have understood correctly what they have told you   5.1e
- retain your notes on file for reference when writing your report.

Where your detail comes from written material, make copies of the material (obtaining permission where necessary) for retention in your files. If you cannot make copies, note carefully where the information can be found. For example, if you are reporting on errors in a financial   5.1e
control system, you must be able to specify exactly where those errors occurred. If you do not have copies of documents which display the errors, you must be able to specify the dates and reference numbers of the transactions in which the errors occurred.

Even if you do not mention these reference points in your report, you must have the detail available in case the facts are disputed. 'I'm sure I had a note of it somewhere' will undo all of the careful work you have done in building up a strong argument. File your supporting notes   3.2
using the same numbering as you do for your report.

d) **Interviewing technique**   Ref

Interviewing technique is an extensive subject, too wide to be covered exhaustively in this report.   App
Fortunately, there are a few questioning methods which will greatly improve your ability to   4I
extract reliable information, and we can deal with them here.

Firstly, be in sympathy with your interviewee. He is much more likely to impart information, and particularly opinions, when he feels that you understand and sympathise with his difficulties and his point of view. This is particularly important when he is wanting to express a derogatory view about his organisation or the authority above him. You may need to probe these adverse views if you are looking for the source of problems in the organisation, and you are unlikely to persuade anyone to talk if you approach him from a hard-nosed authoritarian angle.

Show your sympathy indirectly. Do not say 'I know exactly how you feel' as he will disbelieve you instantly. How could you possibly know? Instead, make some mild comments in agreement with his complaints. 'It seems that people aren't always fully aware of the complexity of your work' is the kind of sympathetic and safe comment likely to show your understanding of his problems. But don't overdo it; he may quote you!

It may be necessary to harden your approach if the interviewee proves difficult, but there is usually a much more effective technique. Cut the interview short (subtly), appear satisfied, and thank the interviewee for his information. Chat to him casually on the way out. A day or so later, contact him and say: 'What you told me has really got me thinking; I'd value your opinion on a couple of related points. Could you possibly spare me a few minutes some time today?' He will perceive that he is now regarded as an authority and his pride will make him ready to tell you everything you want to know from him, and probably a few inside details you weren't expecting. This gentle approach rarely fails.

cont'd

The Report Report
Notes and Observations

d) Interviewing technique (continued)   Ref

Secondly, do not lead the interviewee. People tend to give you the answers which they believe you want to hear, and if you say 'do you always do [a procedure]' they will almost inevitably answer 'yes'. An obvious example of leading the interviewee occurs in interviews with sportsmen, many of whom are not skilled interviewees. Broadcasters therefore pitch them leading questions with the answer contained in the question.

'Do you think Brzhezhinski had a big influence in the second half?' elicits the answer 'Yeah, Brian, I thought Bronski had a big influence in the second half,' thereby giving both the broadcaster and the athlete, if not the listener, an easy ride.

Good sports coverage it may be, but effective information-gathering it is not.

The way to avoid leading the interviewee is by asking **open questions**. Open questions are questions which cannot be answered with 'yes' or 'no'. An open question is easy to ask; just begin with one of the following words:

- how?
- where?
- when?
- who?   (or to whom, with whom, from whom etc)
- what?   (or with what, from what etc)
- which?   (or with which, from which etc)
- why?

Any question beginning with one of the above words has to be answered specifically.

However, you can use a leading (yes or no) question to set up an open question, particularly when you wish to trap a deliberately difficult interviewee:

- Do you always lock the door? ['Yes' - now you've caught him]
- Then how does the foreman get in if you have the only key? [he has to admit to lying]

Which brings us to the last point - incorrect information. When you notice an interviewee giving you information which you know or suspect is incorrect, possibly deliberately, resist the temptation to pick him up immediately on the errors. Appear satisfied with the answers and allow the interview to run its course without putting him on his guard. At the end, when the interviewee has relaxed in the belief that all has gone smoothly, pick him up gently on the anomalies. He will usually have compounded them if he is deliberately misleading you, and have to admit that the information was wrong. If not, use the kind of trap illustrated above.

Even when closing the trap, avoid showing aggression or triumph, and maintain the sympathetic approach. You will gain more information that way, usually with less effort.

e) Justification of opinions and conclusions   Ref

Opinions and conclusions are similar, except that opinions may involve a degree of instinct. However, they are different from facts. You can usually prove facts, but it is seldom possible to prove opinions or conclusions, since they involve a process of deduction, possibly supported by experience, beyond the given facts.

cont'd

The Report Report
Notes and Observations

e) **Justification of opinions and conclusions** (continued)   Ref

You therefore have to provide sufficient factual detail to show that the opinions and conclusions you have reached are justified by your findings and any associated facts. The thread of logic between the facts and the opinions or conclusions must be strong. If there is any gap or weakness in that thread, you must acknowledge it in your report, otherwise you may be held to be negligent if events prove your deductions to be wrong.

Stating that your evidence is incomplete is not likely to be well-received by the addressees. It is only acceptable in reporting terms if it is clearly impossible for you to gain the facts. If the gap in the facts is critical, you should discuss it with the addressees before submitting your report; you may require to have the remit amended.   2.1e

When stating your opinions or conclusions, make specific reference to the facts on which you are basing them. For example: 'In view of the absence of adequate enemy logistics in the area, we consider that the rapid build-up of tanks and infantry in sector H is a feint and we should expect the attack to come from a more heavily supported sector.'

f) **Subsequent reference**   Ref

Consider whether your report will be used after its submission for any of the following:

- a basis for decision-making, rule-setting or operational procedures
- preventive or security measures
- remedial or other actions
- instructions to other people
- study by other people
- general reference

If this is the case, your report will be considerably more helpful if it includes the further   App
information needed for these subsequent purposes. An example in this report is the provision of   4I
a reading list, to cover subjects such as grammar and interview technique, both of which subjects
are too large to be covered in detail in this report.

However, if your report is being produced on a commercial basis on a remit which does not call   App
for this extra information, you may wish to offer it instead as an extra service for an additional   5C
fee. This is best dealt with in the covering letter submitted with your report.

As with all the aspects of the report, put yourself in the readers' shoes when considering the level of detail. And you may have to put yourself in many other people's shoes if you are interviewing to obtain the information. Be patient with them - some of the most difficult people give you some of the best information, and when you get them on your side they sometimes make better allies than the more easy-going people.

Whichever way you obtain the information, you need to be sure it is reliable, and that it specifically justifies your opinions and conclusions.

Once you have determined how much detail you need in your report, you then have to consider how accurate that detail needs to be. To the nearest unit or the nearest thousand (or 0.1million) units, and to what level of qualitative analysis? You may be tempted just to decide this as you go along, but don't. The level of accuracy required may affect the amount of work you have to do, and your client will not pay for time spent analysing information to a degree he doesn't need. Consider and establish the tolerances at the beginning, or you may have some re-working to do.

SUMMARY   Ref

Reporting is about presenting and distilling facts. To be factual, you must avoid:

- numerical and descriptive inaccuracies   2.4b
- reporting facts out of context   2.4b/d
- omitting key facts   2.4b/d
- typographical errors   2.4b
- spurious accuracy   2.4g

You must therefore gather your information:
- from the most reliable sources - noting where there are any doubts   2.4c
- correctly - interviewing without leading, and checking your analysis of written data   2.3d

Even if you have gathered your information impeccably, you can mislead your readers by mispresenting it. Present it correctly and completely.

a) Objectives and significance   Ref

You need to determine the level of accuracy needed to achieve these objectives:

- your report conveys what you intend it to
- key facts and figures are given the appropriate level of impact and meaning
- clients, addressees or other parties specified in the remit are in a position to make appropriate decisions on the basis of your report
- your credibility as a reporter is upheld, and with it your likelihood of gaining more work and no negligence claims
- you do not carry out any unnecessary work (normally at your own expense) by working to an excessive level of accuracy.

If a report is submitted with only one error, that error will be noticed immediately by the most important addressee. Corporate report writers are familiar with the phenomenon of the company chairman flicking idly through the pages of a major report without appearing to pay much attention, then stopping suddenly at some point and saying, 'That can't be right'. Somehow, he finds the one mistake in the whole report.

It is important to recognise that any error, however small, can reduce the impact of the report and the credibility of its author. The larger the report, the more difficult it is to make it error-free, and even experts make mistakes which escape notice. Accuracy is therefore a major   2.4b
consideration.

The Report Report
Notes and Observations

b) Types of reporting inaccuracy   Ref

Reports are liable to five main types of accidental inaccuracy:

- descriptive inaccuracy - something is described incorrectly
- numerical inaccuracy - a figure is incorrectly calculated   2.4 i
- contextual inaccuracy - the facts are correct, but stated in a misleading way
- typographical inaccuracy - a spelling or similar error is usually an obvious mistake, but an incorrect figure is often less easy to identify
- incompleteness - an omitted fact or figure can cause a report to give a different interpretation from that which its inclusion would give.

These inaccuracies can arise at two stages:

- information is gathered incorrectly
- information is gathered correctly but presented incorrectly or in a misleading way (clarity is therefore an essential component of accuracy).

Inaccuracies of commission can be eliminated by careful examination of information in the   5.1e
collection stages, and then careful review, checking and proof-reading in the production stages. 5.3e/g

Inaccuracies of omission are much more difficult to identify. You must:

5.1e
- plan your information needs carefully at the design stage   5.3e/g
- review your information when drafted and think: have you got all the facts?   5.3h
- rely on a third party reviewer, who is more likely to notice an omission.

c) Information from other parties   Ref

Where you rely on any other parties for any of the information you gather for your report, you must determine the degree of reliance which can be placed on that information. If there is any doubt about the reliability of the source you must state it, otherwise the readers will assume a degree of accuracy which has not necessarily been obtained.

Where you use information which has been researched and published by other parties, you must acknowledge the source in your report, for two reasons:

- it is a legal requirement, without which you will be infringing the source's copyright
- you are covering yourself by pointing out that the research behind the information was carried out elsewhere - but stating the source indicates the level of credibility of the information

However, using outside information does not absolve you of any responsibility for the information. You must ensure that any such information is produced by reputable sources of a high enough authenticity to meet your client's needs. This does not of itself prove the accuracy of the information, but if you have used an acknowledged professional source, you have probably exercised reasonable care.

Remember that so-called 'facts', even those with widespread acceptance, can be wrong.

- The Statue of Liberty is not in New York - it is in New Jersey.
- The title 'Fid Def' does not apply to the Anglican faith - it was granted by the Pope.
- Western UK is not bathed by the Gulf Stream - but by the North Atlantic Drift.
- King Canute was not a fool - he was so capable that his courtiers said he could even turn the tide; exasperated, he demonstrated to them that he could not.
- The 'French' rock star Johnny Hallyday is not French - he is Belgian.

The Report Report
Notes and Observations

d) Zero or negative findings   Ref

In any tabular presentation of information it is usually confusing for the reader if only positive findings are presented. Where no finding is reported for any particular category, the reader does not know whether:

- the result for that category is zero
- that category is not applicable to the context of the information
- the result for that category is unknown
- the result for that category has been obtained, but is not available for the report
- the reporter has forgotten to obtain information on that category
- the result has been obtained, but omitted in error.

When presenting a range of findings, you must therefore prove to the reader that all items in the range have been considered. If there are a large number of zero or inapplicable findings, you can deal with them with a note stating that there were no other positive findings than the ones you have stated.

If you have not obtained information on all items in the range, you must report the extent of the shortfall, or the report will purport to be more accurate than it really is.

If you are reporting on something which has not been found or proven, be careful how you report on it. For example, you cannot prove that the Loch Ness Monster does not exist, but you can state (detailing the research you have carried out) that there has not been sufficient evidence found to date to prove that it does exist.

e) Numerical accuracy   Ref

Numerical accuracy is discussed in the statistics subsection. In practical terms, you should report to the level of accuracy which is enough to tell the reader what he needs to know about the items   3.4
you are measuring.

Any less accuracy renders your report ineffective, and any more accuracy is a waste of time: yours and the addressees'. It is also a waste of money - usually yours.

f) Information on residual categories   Ref

Where you are reporting on certain specific categories within a total population of information, it usually reduces your work and makes your report clearer if you account for the residual categories as a single entity. A typical example is a list of territories: Europe, North America, Pacific Rim, Asia, Rest of World (ROW) - ensure that you define these territories in the same way as your client does. The 'rest of' grouping is common in the presentation of statistics,   App
especially where you are only concerned with some of the categories in a population.   3H

You must ensure that the 'rest of' category total is correct by calculating it specifically. If you merely enter a balancing figure to make up the grand total for the whole population, you will fail to detect any error in the specific categories. In the above example, an overstatement in your Europe figure would cause an understatement in your Rest of World figure and vice versa.

Forcing any total by entering a balancing figure is a dangerous short-cut, as it fails to confirm your calculation.

The Report Report
Notes and Observations

g) Spurious accuracy

Ref

Ensure that your report does not purport to achieve accuracy which cannot in practice be achieved. A frequent and annoying example is metric-imperial equivalents such as 'flying at an altitude of 1,500 ft (457.2m)'. This is spurious because 1,500ft is obviously an approximation, but the metric equivalent is supposedly accurate to 0.1metre. The sensible presentation would be '1,500ft (450m)'.

Another example is the quoting of a city population as 4,757,328. No census is ever that accurate, and even if it were, the births, deaths and relocations since the census would make it inaccurate within a few hours. The most accurate figure you could use would probably be 4.76 million. And you should state whether you have measured the municipal area or the total conurbation, and at midday or midnight (i.e. with or without the commute-to-work population).

Any detection by the addressees of spurious accuracy will damage your credibility. How are they to know that all of your other figures are not spuriously accurate?

h) Impartiality

Ref

Your reporting must always be impartial and be seen to be impartial. Impartiality is an essential element of accuracy and of reporting in general.

Even - in fact, especially - if you are writing your report with the express purpose of making certain points (ie you have a strong vested interest in the conclusions) you must demonstrate in the report that you have fully and fairly considered the evidence against your points, and that despite it, your points still stand. This can only enhance the credibility of your report, since you will be seen to have taken due account of the conflicting evidence.

When you are writing to make a point, and you are tempted to ignore some conflicting evidence, ask yourself how strong that evidence is against your point. If it is not strong, there is no danger in including it, but if it is strong . . . should you be making the point at all? In fact, should you be reconsidering your views? If the addressees become aware of conflicting evidence which you have omitted or ignored, this will reflect badly on you and your report in their estimation.

i) Descriptive accuracy

Ref

The section on style deals at length with the question of wording. However, wording must also be used carefully from the point of view of accuracy. Colloquial inaccuracies are common, and fully understood (we say 'boil the kettle' when we mean 'boil the water in the kettle') but these must not be allowed to appear in written reporting. Your narrative has to be accurately worded almost to the point of being pedantic, and your meanings unequivocal.

4.3

If you report frequently, cultivate the habit of speaking accurately so that it becomes instinctive when you write. There is no shortage of humour in doing it, as you become acutely aware of many ludicrous pronouncements by people who are not being accurate in colloquial speech. But be rigorous; don't say 'have your cake and eat it', say 'eat your cake and [still] have it'.

cont'd

The Report Report
Notes and Observations

i) Descriptive accuracy (continued)

Ref

Above all, get names and places right. The news media may report that Britain, America and Holland are sending a peacekeeping force somewhere, but you do not have the luxury of being as casual as that with your reporting. In your report the UK, the USA and The Netherlands are doing the business. There are no such countries as Britain, Great Britain, America or Holland, and for most of the twentieth century there was no such country as Russia; it was one of the fifteen republics of the Soviet Union (USSR).

Geographical accuracy is as hard to achieve as historical accuracy. For example, a reference to 'Europe' can mean the European Union, or merely western Europe (for which there are various definitions), or the whole of Europe, and can also include Turkey and/or Israel, which are geographically in Asia. To complicate matters further, the British frequently refer to Europe in a context which does not include the UK. Combine these possibilities and you have between ten and twenty definitions of Europe. The terms 'Pacific Rim' and 'Asia Pacific' have similar variations. Is Mexico in North or Central America, and does either term include the Caribbean states? When you use such terms you must ensure that you, your clients, your addressees and other readers are all using the same geographical definitions.

App
2C

Beware, though, that there can be conflicts between accuracy and sensitivity. For instance, Sicily is part of Italy and Brittany part of France, but it is more polite to refer to their inhabitants as Sicilians and Bretons respectively. People from regions with a strong sense of identity are more likely to be annoyed at not being identified as such. The subsection on wording also discusses emotive words and accuracy.

4.3f/h

When someone you interview tells you her name is Kathy MacDonald, make sure that it is not Cathy McDonald, Macdonald or M'Donald. If full forenames are needed, check whether it is Catherine, Katharine, Kathryn, Kathleen or some other name. Even John should not be assumed - it could be Jon. And on that subject, it is safer to refer to forenames rather than Christian names.

Real life: *is your client Metcalfe Holdings Limited or Metcalf Holding Ltd? A group chairman and chief executive had to spend a day manually correcting and initialling the corrections in quadruplicate legal documents in which the name of every company in the group had been incorrectly stated, on almost every page. The signature process should have taken a few minutes at the most, and the directors were not amused. Moreover, various related details took several months to resolve. In another group, a senior official was turned off an international flight because his name was spelt wrongly on his ticket and thus did not correspond with the name on his passport.*

Telephone your client's secretary and ask for a list of the names and titles of the personnel and organisations with whom you will be involved, and specify that the list be checked before you receive it. When a name is entered in an information system, it is copied into many other systems and documents and tends to remain in its original form indefinitely. Corrections rarely cover all the systems. Be alert, and be precise.

The above points may sound pedantic, but think about them. Even if you've gathered your information impeccably, you can mislead your readers by reporting sloppily in terms of detail or accuracy. That would be a waste of all your good spadework.

And if you have a team gathering the information for you, brief them thoroughly to ensure that they understand and comply with the parameters governing your information needs.

The Report Report
Notes and Observations

In an ideal world, your client will send you a letter like this, detailing exactly what you have to do for him and when and how. In practice, you may have to make do with a hurried telephone call. But keep trying!

RE Porter
Address

Director of Operations
Client International
Date

Dear Sir

INSPECTION OF OPERATING PLATFORMS

Further to our detailed discussions we confirm that we wish you to carry out a full structural inspection of the following six platforms: KQ154, KQ177, KQ228, KT084, KT085, KV008.

The inspection must be completed between 01 May xxxx and 17 Aug xxxx. You will agree with our Field Operations Manager your proposed transport and accommodation arrangements including access to the platforms and night / bad-weather standoffs.

Our Installations Maintenance Manager will provide you with full plan and elevation drawings of the structures and details of the particular points to be selected for non-destructive testing. The following types of inspection will be required on all platforms:
- magnetic particle inspection
- cathodic potential measurement
- physical survey and still colour photography of specified nodes, risers and clamps, landings, anodes, debris and all lines and cables within a radius of 60 metres from the outside of the jacket
- colour video of selected features
- close-up photography of welds examined by magnetic particle inspection.

Your team will consist of six IGC-qualified inspectors, operating under the rules laid down in the Client International contract safety manual, a copy of which is enclosed. Your team supervisor will contact the Field Controller each morning at 0610hrs on the radio frequency allocated to agree all access to sites and work to be carried out. You will be responsible for providing all accommodation, food and equipment for your inspectors, but they may use site facilities while working on platforms.

You will submit a daily progress report, a blank copy of which is attached, to the Field Maintenance Manager, and liaise with him regarding all operating matters.

Your completed final inspection reports will be in the Client International standard format, a copy of which is attached. You will present five identical copies of each report to the Installations Maintenance Manager no later than 03 Sep xxxx.

The fee for the inspection will be US$780,000 plus sales tax, payable as follows:
- 25% on receipt of the first two satisfactory reports
- 25% on receipt of the second two satisfactory reports
- 25% on receipt of the last two satisfactory reports
- 25% thirty days after receipt of the last two satisfactory reports.

In the event that you are denied access to the sites as a result of Client operations, you will bill Client for each lost half-day at the rate of US$15,000. The amount will be paid on the date of final settlement.

Yours faithfully
Director of Operations

I accept the terms stated above   RE Porter _____   Date _____

If your report project is not covered by a contract, you should prepare an engagement letter, signed by you and your client, to confirm your understanding. The example on page 2 shows the general approach to the document, the style of which will vary according to your client's culture and your relationship with him. The combination of the remit and your engagement letter should define the following matters as precisely as a trading contract would. Your client will probably have additional stipulations of his own (such as the technical qualifications of your reporting team).

Reporting

Objectives, main and subsidiary
Scope:
- overall coverage, and any specific inclusions and exclusions
- general level of detail
- confidentiality (some clients require you to sign a confidentiality agreement - note that sometimes they break their own rules, although they will still expect you to comply with them)
- provenance of information.

Distribution:
- addressees
- colleagues
- external parties.

Format (normally only if it has to comply with client's or addressees' existing reporting conventions)
Signatures and formal matters
Packaging (binders etc), delivery and presentation

Logistics

Access to addressee sites, including any security and out-of-hours clearance
Working space at addressee sites, including confidential communications and document storage
Travel (visas if overseas), meals and accommodation if relevant
Access to addressee information, including use of computer terminals, printers, passwords, e-mail etc
Access to addressee staff for interview (always promised, but seldom provided without difficulty)
Access to addressee office and technical facilities (again, often falling short of promises)
Responsibility for safety, protective clothing etc if sites demand it
Other facilities and arrangements (vehicle access, parking, local contacts, slide projector, etc) to be provided or organised by the addressees

Financial

Liability for payment - is it the head office or the site on which you are reporting, or someone else who is liable to pay you?
Fee and any related taxes, defining specifically how you will charge for:
- collection of information if not provided by client or established sources
- preparation of report
- distribution of report if large number of copies are needed
- travel, accommodation and incidental expenses
- subsequent work, including negotiation and remedial work.

Basis of fees (normally fixed fee for report, but often on time basis for subsequent work)
Penalties (these can go in either direction - you may need a clause stating that delays caused by the addressees will be charged for at a specified rate)
Payment dates (stage payments may be necessary on a long reporting project, and the length of credit should always be stated)

The Report Report
Notes and Observations

Your client has just given you a phone call. He wants you to prepare a proposal to raise UK£4.5M for a factory expansion. He's in too much of a rush to write you a remit, so you'd better prepare a sound engagement letter if you want this project to stay on track. This example is an abbreviated version of a typical letter for this type of assignment.

Financial Director
Client Manufacturing

RE Porter
Address
Date

Dear Tarquin

PROPOSAL FOR FACTORY EXTENSION - NEW PRODUCT LINE

Further to our telephone discussion today, I am delighted to confirm that I shall prepare from the information provided by you and your fellow directors a proposal for the financing of your extension, and shall assist you in the negotiation of the finance with your bankers.

The proposal will be based on the following information provided on the specific instructions of your directors by your development, manufacturing, marketing and finance teams:

- management accounts and related reports for the past three full years and the current year to date
- budget for the current year and rolling three year plan underpinning the budget
- marketing plan underpinning the rolling plan, and all relevant current market analyses
- internal rationale and proposal documents for new product, including market analyses, technical specification, design and build plans and costings
- plans and costings for proposed factory extension, production line and storage and manning
- statutory documents relating to financial structure and current banking arrangements.

I envisage that we can compile the necessary background sections from our existing knowledge of Client, but we shall need to examine documentation regarding licences, leases, contracts, insurance, health and safety, quality standards and personnel management. Please will you ensure that these and any other documents we request sight of are made available within one working day of the request.

My team will be led by Marco Antonio, who has nearly ten years' experience of raising finance in the manufacturing sector. He may have up to four people with him at your factory at one time. Please will you ensure that they have the uninterrupted use of a lockable office with a secure telephone line, and a terminal with access to your financial and manufacturing information systems.

Our work will begin on 17 November 200X and we shall present you with a draft proposal on 13 December 200X. I envisage that after your review and the subsequent amendments, we shall be able to begin negotiations with the bank immediately after the New Year break.

Our fee for the preparation and presentation of the plan will be UK£116,000 plus VAT, exclusive of outlays, which will be charged at our normal rates. After the initial presentation to the bank our negotiation work will be billed to you monthly on the basis of time spent and expenses incurred. All bills are payable within fourteen days of the date of billing.

I stress that while we shall be dealing with the preparation and presentation of the proposal, the responsibility for providing accurate content and meeting the targets set in the plan remains with the directors of Client. I look forward to working with you on this project.

Yours sincerely
RE Porter

Please proceed on the terms stated above. Client _____ Date _____

The Report Report
Notes and Observations

The Report Report
Notes and Observations

Now that you have decided on the content of your report, you have to determine the order in which to present it. Quite apart from the matter of readability, a well-planned sequence can save you a lot of work; you don't have to keep adding explanatory notes referring to other parts of the report. This makes life much easier for the writer and reader alike.

SUMMARY

An effective sequence is one which is logical to the readers, and is based on:

- **an understanding of the addressees' existing knowledge and how to build upon it**
- **an introduction which gives the readers the overall picture from the beginning**
- **a logical progression of detailed information which takes the reader comfortably through the report without having to refer back and forth.**

Ref

3.1b
3.1c
3.1d

a) Objective

Ref

The objective of the sequence in which you structure your report is to present your information to the addressees in a way which builds their knowledge progressively and logically, and which is therefore easy to understand.

To do this, you must introduce the addressees to the main content and findings of the report, to provide a framework for their reading. This is the purpose of the executive summary, and also of the short summary at the start of each subsection.

Thereafter, whenever you give the addressees an important piece of information, you should give the necessary explanation together with the information. If the addressees have to soldier on through the report with important points remaining unexplained until some unknown section further on, they will soon become frustrated. This will greatly diminish the impact of your report, even if your individual points are convincing.

1.3
above

b) Addressee knowledge

Ref

In determining the content of your report, you should already have ascertained what the addressees know already. If not, then do this before you go any further. You have to consider their existing knowledge in deciding not only what to include in your report, but also in what sequence to report it.

2.2b

Even if the addressees are evidently fully aware of the background, it may be necessary for the sake of clarity for other readers to summarise the key points in a separate section, subsection or appendix. This allows the addressees to skip it easily if they wish, but presents a complete report in the eyes of other readers less familiar with the subject. You can alternatively place such a summary in an appendix if it is likely to be a source of irritation to the addressees at the beginning of the report.

3.2k

Do not apologise for including such a summary. An apology suggests that you are being incompetent in some way. Instead, preface the section with a phrase such as 'For the benefit of those not familiar with ... this section outlines ...'

You may also meet cases where the addressees' understanding of a key issue is incorrect, or where you disagree with their perception. In such cases, correct this at an early stage. Keep the correction impersonal, along the lines of: 'It has been commonly understood that [state the perception], but the following figures indicate that ...'

The Report Report
Notes and Observations

c) Introduction
Ref

The sequence within the introduction should not need to vary greatly from that used in this report. There may occasionally be factors relating to the addressees, the remit or the subject which call for a slightly different sequence. Let common sense prevail and above all, ensure that the introduction gives the overall picture from the beginning.

1.1-4

1.3

Where the report has an important numerical content, the same approach is needed in the introduction as for the narrative. The key figures should be quoted in summarised format (probably rounded to a high level) in the executive summary, so that the addressees immediately understand the scale of the subject. You should only include enough figures to support your conclusions and recommendations; the detail can follow in the individual sections.

3.4 f
App
1B

d) Main body of report
Ref

Designing the sequence of the body of the report can be easy or difficult depending on the subject. For example, the sequence of this report selected itself, since it is the chronological sequence through which you have to work to produce a report.

The most likely logics on which to build your sequence are:

- **chronological**: using the order in which events actually happened or are intended to happen
- **by priority**: if you are reporting on a number of alternatives, they should be ranked in the order of relevance to the addressees, such as the order of suitability for their needs, or the order of threat to their activities
- **operational**: following an operational thread or logic
- **inherent**: using a sequence which already exists in the remit or the subject matter

3.2e

Examples:

- **chronological**: the report on a fraud can logically start with the discovery of the fraud, followed by the investigation process and then the findings and conclusions
- **by priority**: the report on a series of options for dealing with a problem can be presented in order of feasibility, desirability, cost or length of time
- **operational**: a proposal to raise finance for a business can describe the business's objectives, its market place, its products, its management and resources, and then present its specific plan to exploit these factors profitably
- **inherent**: a report on a series of social problems in various areas could be arranged by the areas / social strata / social problems existing in the population

App
3A

Whatever sequence you use, you may find as you are writing that you are often having to interrupt your planned flow to explain points. This suggests that part of your sequence may need adjusting. Stop writing and consider whether the explanations and information you are interposing should be put in a section earlier in the report. If you are still struggling, ask a suitable colleague to review your draft report.

5.3h

Remember: you are not writing a murder mystery. The answers should come first, followed immediately by the reasoning, and you will sometimes need explanatory links between points. Some readers may only read the answers, while others may read the full explanation as well. Your report has to be intelligible to the full range of your readers.

The Report Report
Notes and Observations

With your report contents marshalled into a logical order in your mind, it should be easy to put a numbering system to it all. But there are a number of matters to be considered first. A well-thought-out report can be muddied by a confusing or cumbersome numbering system.

SUMMARY   Ref

You must highlight the logic of your sequence by easily understandable numbering.

- Assemble your material into main groups of five or fewer instead of using long lists.   3.2b
- Use a simple, consistent numbering system.   3.2c/d
- If there is already a recognised and logical numbering inherent in the subject, harmonise the
  numbering of the report with the existing numbering.   3.2e
- Do not use continuous numbering if another system is more recognisable.   3.2f
- Make your numbering visible by using large digits in the top right-hand corner.   3.2g
- Use a clear cross-reference system.   3.2h
- If the report is likely to be copied in part, show the section and subsection heading on every page. 3.2j
- Use appendices for diversionary material - but do not use footnotes.   3.2k/l
- When preparing short reports, use the same approach, but in a simpler form.   App
                                                                                                3C

a) Objectives   Ref

The objectives of the numbering system in a report are: Cont-
                                                                                    ents
- to give the reader an immediate feel for the overall shape and logic of the report
- to enable the reader to find any topic in the report rapidly and easily

The second objective is obvious to all, but the first objective, that of conveying the overall form
and logic, is often ignored, resulting in a shapeless morass of a report.   3.2b

b) The rule of fives   Ref

This report consists of 21 subsections which have been grouped into five sections, giving an   Con-
average of four subsections per section. If the subsections had merely been listed as 21   tents
consecutive sections without any grouping, would the form and logic of the report have been as
easily understandable by the reader? Unlikely.

The problem is that the mind cannot easily assimilate a long list of items. You can probably
remember a shopping list of five items without writing them down, but if the list gets longer, you
are likely to forget something. You should therefore divide your report into five or fewer main
sections, and each section into five or fewer subsections. This gives the report an immediately
understandable shape, which gives the reader a sense of comfort and familiarity.

Most subjects for reports can be divided into four or five main sections quite easily and naturally,   App
such as the example of a business plan index at the back of this section. If there are a very large   3A
number of subsections in one section, you can usually split the section logically into two sections.
It may be easier to assimilate six sections of five subsections, than five sections of which one has
ten subsections.

In this report the rule of fives was strictly applied to sections and subsections. But some
subsections, including this one, have many topics with no logical sub-groupings, and the topics
were therefore left as large groups, to avoid having sub-subsections.

cont'd

The Report Report
Notes and Observations

b) The rule of fives (continued)   Ref

Down at the level of detailed topics, it can be difficult to avoid having a larger number. This is not so critical, provided that they are clearly headed and arranged in a logical sequence.

At the end of this section is an example of how headings can be grouped for effect.   App
3B

c) General numbering
Ref

Avoid Roman numerals. They are unwieldy and inconsistent in length (eg VIII, IX, X), and are not universally recognised.

Should you use digits or letters? Letters give you a longer list (26 as opposed to 10), but since we   3.2b
are trying to use small groups it is probably better to rely mainly on digits. They are sequential
by definition, whereas alphabetical order is merely a tradition. However, letters are useful when   Below
subordinated to numbers.

Subsections can be indexed by decimals (such as this section, 3.2) or by letters (such as 3b or 3B).   App
Decimals have the advantage of still being inherently sequential, and therefore give the sequence   3B
a better definition.

When subsections are further divided into topics, many people use a double decimal, under which this topic would be numbered 3.2.3. This is strictly logical but begins to look ponderous, especially if the third number reaches double digits. And 3.2.3 is not so easy to memorise as 3.2c. This report therefore uses a combination of digits, decimals and letters as being the best combination of logic and reader-friendliness.

The author originally envisaged that the appendices would all be at the back of the report. However, the need to provide examples for reference resulted in a larger number of appendices than anticipated, and the author therefore decided to present them at the ends of the relevant sections, closer to their subjects. This meant that an additional numbering stream was needed, and the author chose a simple combination of the section number and a capital letter. Had there been only a few appendices at the very end of the report, they would have been indexed simply   App
by capital letters.   3A

d) Conflicting numbering systems
Ref

There must be only one numbering system, and all references must be to this system. For example, it is confusing to read a report in which the sections and subsections are numbered, but the cross-references are to page numbers. What is the point of setting a carefully defined numbering system and then using a different one for reference?

Some reporting disciplines, notably legal ones, insist that all pages are numbered, to prove that each copy of the report is continuous and complete. If this is necessary (it can be avoided by marking 'Page 1 of 4' etc on subsections of more than one page), cross-references should still be made to subsection or topic numbers, not page numbers. This is because the subsection numbers   above
define the structure and logic of the report and the location of information, whereas page   3.2c
numbers run on a different logic to confirm completeness and record the amount of paper used.

cont'd

The Report Report
Notes and Observations

d) **Conflicting numbering systems** (continued)   Ref

Moreover, section numbers remain unchanged once a report has been finalised, but page numbers can change if different font sizes, margins or paper sizes are used in reproducing the report. If that happens, you have to check the entire report, changing the references to the new page numbers. Most word processing software adjusts the page numbering automatically, but this tends to restrict your choice of layout.

Another difficulty with using page numbers is the treatment of blank pages, section contents pages etc. Should they be numbered or not? Conventions vary, which adds to the potential confusion of using page numbers.

Note that in some reports an occasional page is deliberately left blank (usually but not always to allow a new section to begin on the right hand side). In such circumstances it may be appropriate to print 'This page has intentionally been left blank' to prevent concern that there may be material which has failed to print.

e) **Inherent numbering**   Ref

A report may relate to a subject which already has a recognised inherent numbering system, especially a numbering system used by the addressees in their regular operations. In such a case, the report should if at all possible use the numbering system already established, unless it is patently unsuitable for the report. A common example of this would be an inspection report on several engineering installations which your client has numbered. If the installations are numbered P1, K1, K4 and M3 and normally reported in that order, you should also number your sections P1, K1, K4 and M3.

Real life: A group with nearly 100 subsidiary businesses produced a manual of financial procedures. An internal audit programme ensured that these procedures were followed by the subsidiaries. The internal auditors who reported back to the group office made and filed notes to support their findings.

The index for the audit programme was different from that of the manual, and each auditor compiled his own numbering for his working notes. With three different numbering systems in operation, everything in the programme had to be cross-referred to both the manual and the notes, and the notes had to be cross-referred to both the programme and the manual. To crown it all, the auditors prepared reports which had to be referred to the manual, the programme and the notes. Hard to believe.

The programme and the working papers should have used the same index as the manual. There would then have been no cross-references needed. Good solutions are usually simple solutions, but some people just have to complicate matters.

f) **Non-continuous numbering**   Ref

The practice of corresponding to an existing intrinsic numbering system means that there is no   3.2e
need to adhere to continuous numbering if non-continuous numbers are more easily recognisable. However, you must index the report especially clearly to ensure that the non-continuous numbering is fully understood and that the report is seen to be complete.

Thus if you are writing a report on some aspect of the years 2007, 2009, 2012 and 2015, you should number your sections 07, 09, 12 and 15 instead of 1, 2, 3 and 4. The purists will wince, but the client will like it, since he does not have to remember section numbers.   cont'd

The Report Report
Notes and Observations

f) Non-continuous numbering (continued)   Ref

Real life: *A team of divers was called out urgently to inspect three damaged subsea pipelines. The lines were laid in 12-metre sections over several kilometres of seabed.*

The diving team designated the lines A and B (both large diameter) and X (smaller), and had a report page for each joint. The joints had been numbered by the pipelayers as each section of pipe was welded, and the divers used the joint numbers as the page numbers. Thus page B327 in section B referred to joint 327 on line B, and was instantly recognisable as such. An index at the front listed the joint numbers which had been inspected and provided proof that the report was complete.

The divers only inspected a selection of the joints. For three weeks, they were sent from one location to another without warning. Each night a helicopter took the photographs and the divers' inspection data inshore, where the diving company typed the reports (PCs had not been invented then), inserted the best of the photographs and filed the pages in the report binder in joint number order. Everything was already in the order that the insurers would understand, and no page numbering was needed.At every stage in the project, the report was complete up to the previous night.

24 hours after the last joint was inspected the complete report was on its way to the insurers' office several thousand kilometres away. Impressed at the speed, accuracy and simplicity of the report, they put all their local inspection business to that diving company - all because of a simple, commonsense numbering system, which enabled the report to be complied easily in near-real-time and the client to understand it instantly. And it's the client who pays you.

g) Visibility   Ref

Whichever numbering system you use, make it visible. Anyone in a hurry wants the numbers to be at an outer corner (usually the top corner) of each page in large print. So why do people put them at the centre of the bottom edge in small print? Probably because it was always done that above way, which is the worst reason for doing anything.

h) Cross-references   Ref

If you have a lot of cross-references (references to another part of the report) then put them in a   All separate column at the right hand side of the page, as this report does. That avoids cluttering the text with frequent references in brackets, italics or a different font.

Conversely, if your report has only a few cross-references, it is probably easier to put them in brackets in the text where they arise. Besides, page after page of empty reference columns looks strange, not to mention wasteful.

i) Changes in sequence   Ref

Bear in mind that you may occasionally have to change the sequence of your reporting if you find that the information does not flow easily and naturally. This will mean changing your cross-   3.1d reference numbers. This is easier to do if your references are by section / subsection / topic than if they are by page numbers. You may also insert or remove parts of the report much more easily if you are indexing by sections etc.

The Report Report
Notes and Observations

j) Page headings

Ref

At the risk of being accused of wasting paper, you are better to repeat the section and subsection headings at the top of every page. Because you are producing a report of high quality, readers Above will make photocopies of parts of the report, and it is helpful to them and to you if each sheet copied shows clearly the report and section from which the copy came. In this way you are less likely to be quoted out of context.

More importantly, if your report is confidential, you are more likely to prevent or detect illegal copying if each page is headed.

k) Appendices

Ref

People can become remarkably heated on the subject of appendices. Some say vehemently that appendices should never be used, while others use them extensively. In practical terms, the decision whether or not to put information in an appendix is a simple one.

If a diversion (an example, for example) is a short one which helps explain the point you are making, then put it in the text. A good example often gives a better explanation than the 3.2e/f explanation itself.

On the other hand, if you have a list of examples or other data which reinforce the text but are not necessary to explain it, then place them in an appendix. That gives the reader the choice of looking up the information there and then, or returning to it at a later date for further study. In App the case of numerical detail, it is useful to put summary figures in the text, supported by detailed 4E analysis in an appendix.

It goes without saying that any information which plays no direct part in the flow of text but is included for only for interest must be put in an appendix. Examples are a list of other publications App by the same author, and a list of reference material. 4I

l) Footnotes

Ref

Footnotes are common in books, where there is a single flow of text from beginning to end, but the author wishes sometimes to make a related point or provide information at the foot of the page to which it relates. Footnotes are usually printed in a different font from the main text to distinguish them from the text.

Since a report, although it also should flow, is a series of separate points, there should be no need for footnotes. If a point has to be made, it should be incorporated into the normal indexing of the report. For example, the real-life examples printed in this report in italics are to give practical context to the points being made, and so they are included in the text rather than as footnotes. 3.2 f

One could argue forever on the subject of footnotes and appendices. If in doubt, as with all other aspects of reporting, put yourself in the addressees' shoes and read the report from their point of view and knowledge.

The Report Report
Notes and Observations

m) Short reports   Ref

It is often said, with much justification, that the best reports are those which are presented on
one page. In business or any other area of management, a culture of short, sharp one-page   App
reports is a particularly effective management discipline. It encourages people to communicate   3C
effectively but prevents the communication process from becoming a chore to either the writer SA2-A
or the reader.   SA2-B

The higher up an organisation a report is addressed, the shorter it should usually be. Boards of
large groups of companies will make quite major decisions on the strength of one- or two-page
reports. The boards can do this because they have below them a highly-skilled reporting
capability which ensures that the necessary groundwork underlying the report is properly
completed.

Naturally, short reports do not require the degree of numbering discussed in this section.
Nevertheless, the same principles apply, and a short report with simple numbering (usually 1a,   App
1b, 1c, 2a, 2b etc) is easier to follow and to refer to than one with no numbering.   3C
                                                                                                 SA2

The question of short reports in general is addressed as a special application.

*Whatever you do, keep it simple. Use the numbering logic which relates most easily to your subject
and your addressees, and give them an easy read. And remember that they will later want to read
specific topics again, so they must be able to find them quickly.*

The Report Report
Notes and Observations

With the sequence of your report decided upon and the numbering compiled, you have an effective skeleton for your report. But before you grab your trusty laptop and start rippling your fingers over the keyboard, stop and think about what kind of flesh you want to hang on your skeleton. The overall layout of your narrative is a major factor in both the appearance and the readability of your report.

SUMMARY   Ref

A well laid-out narrative is easier to write and to read than a formless one. The requirements for the narrative in a report are different from those of writing a book or an essay, and include the following considerations:

- **clear alignment of headings and subheadings**   3.3b
- **clearly defined paragraphs of lengths appropriate to the content**   3.3c
- **margins which allow binding, faxing and copying, and also easy reading**   3.3d
- **use of lists where there are a number of individual points to be made**   3.3e
- **use of narrative tables where the points are interrelated**   3.3f
- **variation in length and style of sentences**   3.3g
- **appropriate sizes and styles of fonts**   3.3h
- **appropriate page orientation.**   3.3i/j

a) Objective   Ref

The way in which your narrative is laid out is subject to various considerations:

- to make it as easy as possible to read and assimilate quickly
- to emphasise any relationships between parts of the narrative
- to allow you to write the report easily and quickly
- to make it easy to amend the draft report after each review.   5.3

The above is hardly a revolutionary statement, but many narratives are laid out in such a way as almost to defy easy reading and understanding. In most cases, narrative which is easy to read and understand is also easier and quicker to write.

b) Headings and subheadings   Ref

Arrange your headings on the left of the page (assuming you are reporting in a language written   Above
from left to right). This makes it easy for the reader's eye to flow from the headings to the subheadings to the text, noticing the numbering at the same time.

There are two exceptions, where it is clearer to align headings to the **right**:
- where there is a column of numbers, which are themselves aligned to the right - there are   App
  few more visually annoying presentations than having several columns of figures with the   3E
  headings aligned in the centre or to the left, so that the heading of each column appears to
  refer to the figures in the previous column
- if a column is situated at the right hand edge of a page, it is visually more pleasing to have
  the text and headings aligned to the right, to give a neater edge and overall appearance to   All
  the page, as is done with the reference columns in this report and the presentation example   App
  at the back of this section   3E

Give the greatest prominence to the headings which most need to catch the readers' attention.
These may not necessarily be the 'senior' headings. For example: above
- the heading 'NARRATIVE' at the top of this page is in the largest font
- a fax should have the ADDRESSEE'S NAME in large font, not the word 'fax'

cont'd

THE REPORT REPORT   **3.3**
3. LAYOUT
3.3 NARRATIVE   Page 2 of 6

b) Headings and subheadings (continued)   Ref

Most financial printouts have your company name, which you already know, in large font, and what you want to find quickly (eg an account title) in smaller font - not clever.

Resist any desire to centralise headings on the page, because:

- it interrupts the natural flow of sight described above
- as the whole document is not symmetrical anyway, there is little point in making one small part of it symmetrical.

Where your page is portrait-oriented, such as this page, the heading of the page sits naturally at the top. However, if you are presenting information in landscape format, it is much easier to find the page if the title is at the bottom, ie the outside edge. This layout has the added advantage of keeping the reference at the top right hand corner.   App 3A / App 3D / App 3E

c) Paragraphs   Ref

In general, you should avoid long paragraphs (more than three sentences of average length) unless the content and logic of a paragraph are such that it would impair the flow and meaning of the narrative to split it. If that is so, you should consider presenting the points as a list, to distinguish them clearly.   3.3e

Break your paragraphs where there is a natural step in the logic or the topic. Since you have designed the report by listing the topics to be covered in each subsection, you have already defined the logic trail, and the paragraphs will almost define themselves.

To emphasise a point, give it a paragraph of its own.

The traditional method of marking paragraphs is to indent the first line of each paragraph, and this is still used in books, wherein the narrative has a single overall flow. However, a report, while having a flow, is chiefly a succession of individual points. You will therefore achieve a greater impact by using the block format (also referred to as Civil Service style in the UK) as used in this report, where paragraphs are separated more distinctly, by missing a row of text, without any indentation.   All

This block style of typing also uses the convention that full stops (periods in the USA) are usually not used for abbreviations. This gives a smoother, less fussy appearance.   All

d) Margins   Ref

If the addressees are likely to want to make notes on the report, they may welcome a wide margin. Ask them. If they do not need a wide margin for notes, observe the following points in setting your margins.

- Leave an adequate width for binding or punching.
- If printing on both sides, ensure that the binding margin is on the correct side for left- and right-hand pages (your word processing software should do this).
- If setting up a landscape-oriented page, place the punching / binding margin at the **top**, so that the page is on the nearer side of the folio to the reader.   App 3A
- Ensure that after the binding width the margin on the inside edge matches the free space on the outside edge, to give the page a balanced appearance.
- Leave sufficient space around all four edges to allow for loss of image on photocopying or faxing.   cont'd

The Report Report
Notes and Observations

d) Margins (continued)   Ref

The above points may seem obvious, but there are an astonishing number of allegedly intelligent people who type or write close to the edges of a sheet, only to have part of their output obliterated by punch-holes or photocopying. Most financial computer printouts have this defect, and to make matters worse the left hand column almost always contains the date or reference number. You therefore cannot find the transaction you are looking for, because the reference has been punched out. One is occasionally tempted to recommend a similar fate for the designer of the report.

The ideal width of a margin is a matter of personal preference. It should be wide enough to satisfy the parameters listed above, but not so wide that it is a waste of paper. Overall, the appearance of the page should be professional and pleasing.

The other factor governing the size of a margin is the size of font used. If the font is small, there   3.3h
will be a large number of words on a single row, which may make the text difficult to read, and require wider margins, or two columns of text.

Most report-writing is now done on word processors, using software that can justify (ie align) the text on the right hand side as well as the left. Use this for your main text as is done in this report;   All
it looks immeasurably neater.

However, if you are writing in **note form**,   4.2k
your notes will be clearer if you begin each new line
at a natural break in the narrative
as has been done in this instruction
(this applies particularly to e-mails).

e) Lists   Ref

Where a sentence or a paragraph includes several points, break it up and present the points as a list. This layout is more effective because:

- it highlights that there are several different points contained in that part of the text
- it shows more easily whether the points are individual and should be considered separately, or whether they are related and have to be considered together
- it enables the reader to consider the points individually, clearly and thoroughly
- it communicates to the addressee the thought you have put into the points
- it creates a clearer thread of thought through the points
- a list is easier to write than a long sentence or paragraph
- it enables you to change the sequence of the points more easily if needed
- if you are a student, the examiner will give you a separate mark for each point.

The legal profession is sometimes guilty of incorporating a string of points in a long sentence, making the points difficult to assimilate. The same points set out in a list would be less intimidating and much clearer, and better for the reputation of the profession. The general public regards long sentences as an unnecessary and (amongst habitual conspiracy theorists) perhaps deliberate complication.

If the points in a list are likely to be discussed or referred to individually, number them. Otherwise, bullet points (the style used here) will usually suffice. It may be necessary to end each point except the last with 'and' or 'or', to establish whether the points are additive or alternative. If, as in this report, there is no such distinction, the convention is that the points are additive unless they are specifically stated to be alternatives.

The Report Report
Notes and Observations

f) Tables   Ref

Where a narrative contains a number of points which are related to each other in clearly defined
ways (eg cause and effect; observation and recommendation), set the narrative out in a table so   App
that the relationships amongst the points are easily visible. This gives you the advantages of both   3D
narrative format and graphic format, and the effectiveness of this method is limited only by your
creativeness.

Laying out text in a table usually necessitates using landscape orientation of the page. Some   App
organisations use the landscape format as standard for internal reporting.   3D

g) Sentences   Ref

Long sentences may be necessary to express complex points involving several factors, in which
one part of the sentence expresses an argument which is qualified, expanded or limited by other
parts, but longer sentences require greater concentration on the part of the reader. This can soon   3.3e
become wearing, especially when long sentences are used consecutively, giving the reader little
or no respite from the writer's convoluted chain of thought, particularly when the sentence
construction is clumsy. Moreover, in long sentences, there is a greater danger of grammatical   4.4b
errors such as hanging clauses and tautology, which may cause the meaning of the sentences to   App
be quite different from that intended, which again strains the concentration of the reader.   4E

Short sentences are useful for emphasis. You should not use more than two consecutively.
Children use short sentences. They become painful to the reader. The short sentences, that is.
Children do too, sometimes. In fact, most times. The stop-go effect is hard on the reader. It does
not reflect well on your intellect, either.

The answer, of course, is to vary the length of your sentences. Any sentence of more than three
clauses is in danger of becoming confusing, but a reasonably long sentence will hold the reader's
attention if the sentence is well structured. The sentences also have to be smoothly linked. If each
sentence does not follow in a natural logic from the previous one, the reader will probably have
to re-read passages to follow the thread.

In his gripping novel 'Complicity' the author Iain Banks has a chapter consisting of one sentence   4.2c
of two words. The sentence speaks volumes, and the two words form a pivotal point in the story.

If you are not a natural writer of narrative, it is not a skill you will acquire overnight. Until you
can lay out your narrative instinctively, take the simple approach.

- Concentrate on writing your narrative in short sentences.
- Review the sequence of the sentences to ensure that you have reported the items in the most
  understandable order.
- Then scan the sentences to see which ones can be most naturally combined to form longer
  sentences (it is easier to join short sentences than it is to break up long ones).

In this way you may even achieve a more readable narrative layout than a fluent writer who takes
less care because he writes more instinctively. And you will rapidly improve.

The Report Report
Notes and Observations

h) Fonts (type faces)   Ref

Fonts are not just a matter of personal preference; many factors should be considered.

The more senior your addressees, the larger the font you should use, because:

- people's near sight deteriorates as they grow older, and they become impatient with small print (some people also have difficulty with their pride when their optical faculties diminish, and small print will not endear you to them)
- senior people have a shorter attention span with regard to detail, and a smaller font smacks of detail (in fact a larger font tends to make you use more economical wording to avoid taking up space, so it achieves two objectives)

FOR REASONS WHICH ARE NOT READILY APPARENT, THE BRITISH TEND TO USE UPPER CASE (CAPITAL) LETTERS MORE THAN OTHER NATIONALITIES. UPPER CASE LETTERS USED FOR MORE THAN ONE OR TWO LINES ARE MORE DIFFICULT TO READ THAN LOWER CASE LETTERS, EXCEPT SOMETIMES WHEN THE LOWER CASE IS HANDWRITTEN. YOU ARE TIRING ALREADY. YOU SHOULD THEREFORE RESTRICT THE USE OF UPPER CASE TO MAIN HEADINGS AND ABBREVIATIONS.   3.3c
EVEN LARGE NOTICES ARE MORE EASILY READ IN LOWER CASE.

Which font should you use? It is your choice - here are some popular ones, all of them on Microsoft software:

- Fonts such as **Times New Roman** have been used for decades, but they tend to look bookish. They may, however, be preferred by institutional addressees who have a strong sense of tradition and authority - if so, give them what they like.

- Many modern companies favour **Comic Sans MS** for its informal look, but it takes up more width than most fonts, and is therefore less suitable for tabulated information. As its name suggests, it lacks gravitas.

- **Arial** is simple and uncluttered, and is the default font on the majority of the world's personal computers. It is the easiest font to work with in any form of graphics or tables, being economical on space, especially with numbers. For this reason, the appendices in this report have been presented in Arial. In narrative, it suffers from understated punctuation marks and occasional lack of distinction between letters - for example: modern (MODERN) and modem (MODEM).

- **Tahoma** gives better distinction than Arial, but uses more space for numbers.

- Arial narrow is similar to Arial, but has the advantage of fitting a greater number of characters into a given width of paper - especially useful for fitting narrative into the boxes of a detailed table, or into column headings. It suffers from Arial's disadvantages noted above.

- `Courier New` has been used for many computer applications and although relatively wide, has a major structural advantage: all characters (e.g. 'i' and 'w') have the same width - the characters can thus be perfectly vertically aligned

For *The Report Report*, the author abandoned his normal usage of Arial, on recurring advice that a font with serifs (the little 'feet' on the letters) is easier to read at length. The font used here is **Calisto MT**, chosen for its classic appearance, its clear definition, and the fact that it virtually matches Arial for economy of space. The font size for this book is 10pt, although a slightly larger size (as here - 11pt or here - 12pt) would probably be used for most reports.

The vertical spacing used in this report is single-line.   cont'd

The Report Report
Notes and Observations

h) Fonts (type faces) (continued)   Ref

Variations of font for emphasis are the choice of the writer. We have already relegated UPPER CASE prose to headings and abbreviations, while <u>underlining is visually disruptive and can look</u>   above <u>amateurish</u>. Using a larger font of the same type can give you rows of inconsistent depths, and shading the background can cause blotches on faxing and copying. Colours disappear on most faxes and copiers.

The best (and of course simplest) forms of visual emphasis are therefore **bold** and *italics*, both of which provide contrast without undue disruption.

If you are writing in italics, reverting to standard (roman) font for emphasis *looks a little strange.* You are therefore probably better to use **bold** for emphasis, whatever the font.

Remember, though, that you should achieve most of your emphasis by careful choice of words   4.2j and sentence structure. Use changes of font sparingly, otherwise they will become an annoyance   3.3g

i) One side or both sides?   Ref

In this age of chattering political correctness, you may be a little reluctant to publish a substantial report on one side of the paper only. It does appear to be an unacceptable waste of resources, including money, but it has some practical advantages:

- the reader can make notes on the blank side (left-handers will appreciate this)
- there is no need to keep swapping margin widths depending upon whether text is on the verso (printer's term for left) or recto (right) side; most software helps with this, but it is by   3.3d no means infallible, especially when your report is in several files
- print runs on a standard photocopier are much easier - the number of spoiled sheets rejected in double-sided printing sometimes exceeds the theoretical saving achieved by using both sides
- you avoid any difficulties with print-through of type from the other side of the paper.

j) Portrait or landscape?   Ref

Conventional narrative pages are generally oriented portrait-style, but tabulated narrative usually   3.3 f fits more easily into the landscape orientation, as do most numerical presentations and many   App graphical ones. Do not automatically assume that you should use one or the other; consider how   3E you can best present your information and use whichever orientation gives the more impact.   App
                                                                                                     3D
Beware, though, that frequent changing between portrait and landscape may irritate readers. Such changes may at times be unavoidable, but keep them to a minimum.

A well presented narrative layout will immediately predispose your readers towards you. As with the numbering system, keep it simple. Apart from that, the only limitation is your imagination.

The Report Report
Notes and Observations

Having decided how to set out your narrative, now give some thought to the presentation of figures. The layout of any figures should complement the layout of the narrative, so you have effectively chosen your fonts, margin sizes etc already. But figures, or statistics as they are more menacingly known, bring presentation problems all of their own. Read on.

SUMMARY   Ref

To present statistics effectively in support of your narrative, you must:

- use the level of accuracy needed to prove your points to the addressees   3.4b/d
- lay them out in a logical sequence, typically from base figures to calculated results   3.4c
- use appropriate and clearly stated units of measure   3.4e/h
- quote them consistently when they appear in more than one place   3.4g
- use appropriate base figures as a benchmark for comparison of your figures   3.4i
- state the sources and degree of provenance of the figures   3.4j

a) Objective   Ref

The objective of providing statistics is always the same, whether the numbers are of scientific, military, social, financial or any other type. They are presented to demonstrate clearly a situation which has existed, or currently exists, or is expected to exist, by quantifying the facts or expectations underlying that situation.

The essence of statistics is therefore not the numbers themselves, but the story which they tell. Numbers are there to be used:

- to form your arguments, opinions and conclusions
- to support and quantify them
- to enable the users to decide what actions should be taken to make the best use of opportunities, or to prevent or cure problems.

It is therefore seldom useful to present statistics on their own. Since their function is to support the narrative points which are being made, virtually every set of figures should be accompanied by a commentary which interprets them.

b) Selection   Ref

You have to present your statistics in the way which best supports the points you are making in your report. There may be a conventional way of presenting the figures, but if that does not achieve your purpose do not hesitate to use another format. However, do not doctor the statistics themselves; you must use proven figures.

In selecting which figures to present and how, you need to consider the following:
- the extent to which the addressees are used to dealing with figures
- the extent to which they are already familiar with the facts being quantified
- which figures are most important to them
- the level of detail which is relevant to them (in general, the more senior the addressees, the   2.2c
  more the numbers have to be in summary form)
- the figures which are most important to you in supporting your narrative
- the trail of distillation and calculation from the general figures (e.g. market statistics)   3.4c
  through the analysis process to the statistics you are using to prove your point.

cont'd

The Report Report
Notes and Observations

b) Selection (continued)   Ref

Designing a table of statistics is thus a miniature version of designing the whole report. You have to go through the same processes of questioning.

- What do the addressees want to know?   2.1b
- What do they know already?   2.2b
- How do you determine the content and layout of the figures to make your points as clearly as possible?
- How do you interpret and summarise them in your narrative?

c) Presentation   Ref

Where you are quoting individual statistics, they can be included in the body of the narrative where they occur. If there is some supporting analysis available which is not necessary for understanding the text, it can be presented separately in an appendix or other location, and referred to in the text.

Where you have to present a collection of statistics from which certain key figures or ratios lead to conclusions, then you should follow this simple procedure.

- Present the base data first.
- Secondly, present any related data in logical sequence (there may be choices of logic, such as the order in which to set out costs in a financial statement).
- Then present any incidental data (data which is relevant to your findings, but not directly related to the base data).
- Next, present your distillation of key facts distilled from these related figures (such as the percentage of net return on a product after manufacture and marketing costs).
- Finally, present the results (ie what you are seeking to demonstrate) as the bottom line (hence the use of the phrase 'the bottom line' to describe the most important fact in a set of circumstances).

This sequence works for most types of statistical presentation. For example:

Statistical field	Management accounts	Medical survey
Base data	sales for period	total population
Related data	cost of making & selling	people suffering specific ailment
Incidental data	overhead costs	social factors
Distillation	cost ratios & variances	percentages of people affected
Result	net profit for period	identification of people likely to suffer

Remember that just because you are presenting base data, it does not mean you have to present all of it. For example, in presenting a company's sales and costs of sales you would perhaps show only the totals of its main product groups. However, you would normally have available (either elsewhere in your report or in a separate document which can be provided if needed) the detailed analysis of those key figures.
App
3E

Design your layout, lines, font sizes and styles to give emphasis to the key figures. There are many ways of doing this, but choose one which looks robust and uncluttered. The appendices show examples which have been consistently well received by many types of addressees.
App
3F/G

The Report Report
Notes and Observations

d) Level of detail   Ref

Into what level of detail should you go? Many report writers find this difficult to decide, but the answer for statistics is the same as it is for narrative detail.

You go into just as much detail as is required to prove your arguments conclusively, and no more.

You can hedge your bets quite easily, however, by always presenting figures from the top of the information pyramid and having the underlying detail available level by level. The addressee can therefore delve as deep as he needs to. Many people like to read a report straight through once   App
to understand the overall thrust and tenor of it, and then revisit it in detail to understand the   1B
underlying facts and mechanics of it.

e) Units of measure - size   Ref

You have to choose units of measure in the same way as you have to decide on the level of detail. The measures must be just accurate enough to enable the reader to understand and accept the points you are making.

For example, if you are reporting on a project costing EUR 43 million, your key figures should probably be to the nearest EUR 0.1 million. It will be extremely irritating to the addressees if you present all of your figures to a single Euro, for two reasons:

- they will be swamped in digits, as many as eight at a time, which detract from the impact of the figures
- the detail will show spurious accuracy, since the costs of a project of that size will not be   2.4g
  calculable to that precision

A useful guide in presenting figures is the rule of threes. Avoid using more than three digits in   App
any one figure unless it is necessary, except for the overall total, which can run to four digits. The   3E
readers will appreciate your simplicity and clarity and you can provide the exact figures in an appendix if needed. In the example below, the miles travelled in each region make little impact on the reader, as there are too many digits to assimilate. As soon as they are rounded to 0.1 million miles, they become easy to digest, and the figures are still detailed enough to enable useful interpretation.

Passenger miles travelled	Miles	Million miles	
Americas	47,452,098	47.5	Three digits
Europe & Africa	28,303,115	28.3	Three digits
Asia & Australia	36,047,074	36.0	Three digits
World	111,802,287	111.8	Total - four digits

You will sometimes have figures of greatly differing size in the same table. Try as far as possible to use the same unit of measure throughout, as it can be confusing to read some figures in one unit, eg 0.03M (million), and other figures of the same commodity in a different unit, eg 3K (thousand). However, if the difference in size is so great that you need to use different units, then expressing small figures as percentages of the large ones to which they relate can be helpful to the readers.

In narrative, it is conventional to write the figures nil to twenty as words, and 21 and above as   App
digits. In a table they are all in digits, with negatives usually in brackets.   3E

The Report Report
Notes and Observations

f) Roundings   Ref

Rounding figures down to a few digits as described above can give you some strange results if you are not careful. Consider the following example of expenditure over three months, where your report is rounded to the nearest US$1,000:

	Month 1	Month 2	Month 3	Total	
Expenditure US$	1,540	590	510	2,640	exact
Expenditure US$000	2	1	1	4	rounded
Seasonality	58%	22%	19%	99%	

Each month is accurately rounded, but the total of the roundings (US$2,640) is not the same as the rounding of the total (US$4,000). And the percentages do not total 100%.

The golden rule of rounding is that you must always round to the correct end result (in financial statements that is always the closing balance sheet position). There are three ways of dealing with the US$000 figures. Firstly, you can round to the cumulative total, instead the monthly total, to the nearest US$1,000 (shown as US$K here for brevity).

Rounding to cumulative:	Month 1	Month 2	Month 3	Total	
Expenditure US$	1,540	590	510	2,640	exact
Cumulative US$	1,540	2,130	2,640		exact
Cumulative US$K	2	2	3		rounded
Expenditure US$K	2	0	1	3	rounded

Alternatively, you can round instead to the nearest US$100 (i.e. 0.1 of US$1,000).

Rounding to 0.1:	Month 1	Month 2	Month 3	Total	
Expenditure US$	1,540	590	510	2,640	exact
Expenditure US$K	1.5	0.6	0.5	2.6	rounded
Seasonality	59%	22%	19%	100%	adjusted

Rounding to a more accurate level gives a more sensible result in this particular case, but what level you use may depend on any other figures to be rounded. Note that the seasonality for the largest month (1) has been rounded up to bring the total to 100%.

However, it is apparent from the small exercises above that the process of rounding a large table of figures correctly could take longer than compiling the figures themselves. There is a third solution. If it is acceptable to your client, you can cope with this problem by a note stating 'Figures may contain decimals which are not displayed'. This may seem trivial, but if an addressee notices that rounded figures do not total correctly, why should he believe that any other figures are correctly calculated?

The Report Report
Notes and Observations

g) Recurring figures   Ref

Where the same figure appears in more than one place, ensure that it is the same in each case. This may seem obvious, but it is easy to have slight variations in figures when they appear in different tables, particularly where rounding is involved. An addressee looking at a statistic of 44 on one page and seeing the same figure reported as 43 on the next page will not have much confidence in your reporting.   3.4 f

h) Units of measure - type   Ref

You must always state the units of measure you are using, and state them in a practical place. A currency sign against every figure in a table is unnecessary, fussy and annoying. Stating the units at the beginning of the report is neat and economical, but does not allow each table to be viewed on its own. Since tables are often photocopied separately from a report, each table should show the units used.

Where a table uses more than one unit, there is usually a dominant unit. The easiest way to deal with this is by noting 'All units in [say] tonnes except where stated' at the top of the report. You then only need to annotate figures using different units (for example, percentages or numbers of people). It usually helps if numbers which are not in the dominant unit are visually differentiated, by printing them in italics for instance.   App 3E
                                                                          App 3E

Where you have to annotate non-standard units in a table, try to do it as economically as possible. It is easier to for the writer and the reader if you mark the units at the head of a column or the beginning of a row than if you mark them on every figure. The exception is percentages; it usually helps to use the % sign on each percentage except where percentages themselves are the dominant unit of the table. This is to emphasise that, for example, 52.3% is not 52.3; it is 0.523.   App 3E
                                                                          App 3E

Ensure that your readers are quite clear as to what measurements you are using. Using the proper abbreviations is an essential part of this, and some abbreviations can have a variety of meanings in different contexts. The letter M or m is an abbreviation for miles, metres, millions and thousandths. Some abbreviations are written in Greek letters, which may not be possible to print with the equipment you or your printers are using. In such cases use alternatives and explain them to your readers.

Remember that there are still some countries which use non-metric measurements, the USA being the most prominent. Moreover, the USA uses some measurements which have the same names as Imperial measures but are different in value - gallons are the most common of these. Clarify such matters in your report.

There are other areas of confusion. For instance, air and sea navigation use nautical (sea) miles which represent minutes of latitude, instead of land miles. All aircraft altitudes are measured in feet, but atmospheric pressure, by which altimeters work, has a variety of measurements. This is not a trivial issue; confusion over altitude and barometric pressure measurements in metric and imperial units has resulted in deaths in several air accidents.

Confirm beforehand which units and abbreviations are suitable for your addressees.   4.2 1

The Report Report
Notes and Observations

i) Comparisons   Ref

For a statistic to be meaningful, you almost always have to compare it with another figure which
provides a basis of understanding. For example:

- If you state that in the last ten years the population of country A has grown by 13 million,
  and that of B by 16 million, you are indicating that B has grown faster.
- But if ten years ago, country A had a population of 30 million and B had one of 70 million,
  then the growth rate per decade of A (43%) has been much higher than that of B (23%) even
  though the increase in its absolute population is smaller

The figures only become meaningful when they are compared with the benchmark of the earlier
figures. They would be even more meaningful if they were tabulated.   3.4c

More often than not, the use of percentages and ratios is more important than the base numbers
themselves. The use of intelligent comparisons is therefore a vital part of the presentation of
statistics, and also of forming your opinions and conclusions.

Take for instance the tonnage of a chemical sold in three regions over two years. From these six
figures we can develop useful comparisons: each region's share of the total market in each year,
and the changes in volume and market share year-on-year.

Sales in tonnes		Americas	Europe	Other	Total
200X	Volume	690	487	177	1,354
	market share	*50.9%*	*36.0%*	*13.1%*	
200Y	Volume	804	662	203	1,669
	market share	*48.1%*	*39.7%*	*12.2%*	
Change	Volume	16.5%	35.9%	14.7%	23.3%
	market share	*(2.8%)*	*3.7%*	*(0.9%)*	

Think - what point are you trying to make with your figures? What situation, trend or other
aspect is important to the reader:

- the total sum?
- the change in the total sum?
- the change in the total sum compared with the change in another sum?
- the change in the total sum compared with that in another sum in a fixed period?
- the change in the total sum compared with that in another sum in a fixed period compared
  with the same calculation in another area?

and so on - you must be clear about what you are trying to demonstrate before you can present
your figures meaningfully.

Examples of figures with which you can make meaningful comparisons are:

- the equivalent figure for a different period
- the equivalent figure for a different commodity, product, person, department, business,
  industry, market, region, country etc
- a related figure for the same period (e.g. operating costs of a business are commonly
  compared with the sales value and expressed as a percentage thereof)
- the budgeted, forecast or permitted figure
- the best or worst result previously recorded
- the figure quoted by other sources (which you are corroborating or disputing)
- a combination of the above (e.g. costs as a percentage of sales compared with the same
  percentage achieved elsewhere)   cont'd

The Report Report
Notes and Observations

i) Comparisons (continued)   Ref

Comparison also affects the amount of work you have to do. Where the base figures for
comparison relate to markets, industries, regions etc as a whole, they often take longer and cost   3.4c
more to obtain than the detailed figures on which you are reporting. You can perhaps analyse a
company's sales in a few hours, but how long will it take you to obtain reliable figures for the
whole of that industry? And when the information arrives, will it be analysed in the way in which
you need it for comparison? For example, external market research organisations may analyse
sales into quite different sectors from the ones which you need to use for your internal analysis.

We are all familiar with situations where a person quotes a statistic for effect, and we are not sure
whether to reply 'As big as that?' or 'As small as that?' because the person has not given any
benchmark by which to judge the statistic. Do not make the same mistake in your reporting.

j) Provenance   Ref

How reliable are your figures? Your addressees are entitled to know the extent to which they can
depend on them. Moreover, if any of your figures come from sources outwith your control, you
do not want to be blamed for any errors or distortions therein (it follows that it is always best to
use your client's own figures if they are suitable for your purpose).

You must therefore state the source of each set of figures and the basis on which it has been
obtained. If all of the figures are from the same source, such as the examination of the records of
an organisation, it is normally sufficient to state this in the scope of the report. If different figures
come from different sources, you should note the sources and bases on the tables, and not at the
edge, so that if a table is copied the sources and bases are copied with it.

The significance of quoting the source is not just one of responsibility. It also indicates who has
copyright to the information and how reliable it may be (the assumption being that figures from
a reputable source should be more reliable than others). Reliability also depends on the method
of gathering figures. For example, were figures obtained from a small sample or from a complete
count, and how and to what degree of accuracy were they measured?

If you do not state these matters clearly, you may be held responsible for inaccuracies which you
did not commit.

*Intelligently presented statistics illuminate. Carelessly presented statistics can confuse or mislead,
and may result in your incurring a liability as a result of actions taken on the basis thereof.*

The Report Report
Notes and Observations

As with statistics, the function of graphics is a supportive one. They are not an end in themselves, but must support the points you are making by giving them clarity and emphasis. Graphics are not an excuse to dazzle people with your skill at using some software package, although many report writers appear to be desperate to do this.

SUMMARY

Ref

Graphics are like statistics - they are only there to make your points clearer, and the story which they tell is more important than the graphics themselves. The philosophy of using them is therefore:

3.5a

- only use them if they genuinely are the most effective method of presentation   3.5d
- first set out your numerical factors in a table, in which the base is the independent variables   3.5d
- if the table is clear in its own right, use it - if not, select the most appropriate graphic to make it clearer   3.5d
- harmonise the presentation (fonts, layout etc) of the graphic with your narrative to maintain your 'house style'   3.5e

Examples of suitable and unsuitable graphics are contained in the appendices at the end of this section   Apps 3H-O

a) Objective

Ref

The human brain learns 80% by sight, and 20% through the other senses. It follows that the more visual your report is, the more impact it will have on the reader. The purpose of graphics is therefore to maximise the visual impact of your presentation.

However, many types of information do not lend themselves to graphic presentation. These largely comprise linear themes which do not involve:

- comparisons or relationships amongst qualities
- comparisons or relationships amongst quantities.

For example, in a general discussion of the problems arising from addressee culture, we can do little graphically but lay out the narrative in numbered paragraphs.   4.1b

However, when we discuss specific interpretations of various cultural statements, we have an element of comparison, and can tabulate our interpretations against the statements. Tabulated narrative is the simplest form of graphic - more effective than straightforward narrative, economical in space and relatively easy to devise. Moreover, designing the table usually helps to clarify the thinking of the reporter.   4.1b   App 3D

When the comparative discussion involves quantities, we have two choices:

- present a table of narratives (usually just headings) and the related numbers
- present the quantities in a pictorial, analog form (a true graphic).

In deciding which presentation to use, consider as always the status of your readers. When reporting to a marketing department, do not present a pie chart showing home sales of 30% and export sales of 70%. Why not? Because anyone not numerate enough to understand 30% and 70% from the figures alone should not be in marketing. But when you have a larger number of fields and variables the relationships amongst them become harder for even the most numerate readers to assimilate, and that is where a well-designed graphic is the ideal method of presentation.   App 3H

So the objective of this section is to consider what makes an appropriate graphic.

The Report Report
Notes and Observations

b) Points to ponder   Ref

Presenting information in graphic form is no different from presenting it in numerical, tabular or narrative form. You have to be quite clear before you start just exactly what information you are trying to present, and how the reader is likely to interpret it.

Unfortunately, graphics have become a fashion item. Addressees are often demanding information in graphic form even when it patently does not meet their needs. The manual of a recent software package tells you that graphics will add 'more pizzazz' to your reports. Whether it improves your reports it does not say, and the author finds that graphics often distract attention from the figures themselves.

Most graphics are presented to people who are numerate, and who will therefore understand more from a table of figures in many cases. You should therefore only use graphics when they are genuinely the most effective (ie clear) method of presentation.

The size of lettering and numbering is normally small on graphics, because of the amount of detail being presented on the pictorial spread. This makes graphics particularly difficult to read when presented on a screen. Most of us have at some time yawned our way through slide after   SA1
slide of overcomplicated graphics quite illegible to an entire audience. Keep it very simple.

c) Types of graphic   Ref

The most popular types of graphic and the applications for which they are most effective are shown below. There is an example of each type at the end of this section.

Type	Useful applications	
pie chart	*shows individual portions of a total 'pie' - useful for presenting to the hopelessly innumerate, but most people understand a table of percentages better*	App 3H
isometric pie chart	*avoid it - it can show a small percentage as having a greater area than a large percentage*	App 3H
line graph	*a good simple way to show the trend between one variable and another, and to compare several such relationships - but watch what happens between points*	App 3I
bar graph	*shows similar same information to a line graph - but used for static figures rather than a progressive trend*	App 3J
stacked bar graph	*shows the same information as a bar graph, but with the bars stacked on each other instead of side-by-side*	App 3K
Gantt chart	*good for showing how a series of related activities run - even better if instead of using bars you use figures to denote man-days, costs etc*	App 3L
map	*outline only - useful for giving a visual understanding of territories, areas and distances, especially if annotated with key statistics relating to the territories*	App 3M
process flow chart	*usually the clearest way to describe a process, provided that it is clearly annotated and laid out in the order of flow of the process*	App 3N
other diagram or picture . . .	*its effectiveness depends entirely on the quality and suitability of the diagram picture - clear diagrams and pictures are very helpful to the reader*	App 3O

The Report Report
Notes and Observations

d) Using graphics effectively   Ref

Except where you are using a flow chart, diagram or picture, the specific purpose of a graphic is to illustrate a numerical relationship. Therefore to select the most appropriate presentation you have to consider exactly the relationship which you are trying to demonstrate. The key questions are:

- which quantities constitute the essence of the topic you are dealing with?
- which quantities form the base (the independent variable) against which you want to compare the main quantities?
- what kind of relationship are you wanting to show (ie change in total quantity, change in mix, change in percentage against the base - by area or time, etc)?

Set out base quantities (called the independent variables) in a horizontal row. Above or below each base quantity, create a column showing the quantities relating to the topic of your graph, as they apply to that base quantity. Then add in any percentages (eg percentage of the base quantity or percentage increase from one column to the next) which are needed to highlight the relationship. Add a short narrative at the beginning of each row.   App 3K

On reviewing this table, you will find in many cases that it demonstrates the point you are making quite clearly, without the need for graphics. But if you are not satisfied, try one or more of the graphic layouts and see if it is likely to improve the reader's understanding. If so, use it.   App 3K

Remember that the independent variables are always presented on a horizontal axis. That is a worldwide convention, and you will confuse people if you use a different layout.   App 3K

e) Compatibility   Ref

If you are thinking of using photographs, colour or any other presentation technique which may require special facilities to reproduce, consider first how the report is to be distributed. If it is to be copied elsewhere, ensure that they can reproduce the photos and the colours you are using, and that the readers will not be presented with illegible smudges. Check that your addressees can distinguish colours, especially green and red. Check beforehand that the colours you use match any colour conventions used by your addressees (regional and departmental colour codes are quite common).

If you are using software for your graphics, you may find that it comes in a different presentational format from that of your report. Consider whether the graphics format clashes with your report style, or whether the differences enhance the impact of the graphics, and make any necessary amendments. Your graphics should appear as an integral part of your report, and not as something you have tacked on as an afterthought merely to impress people.

This report presents the appendices, which contain many tables and graphics, in Arial font to illustrate its suitability for those uses. The report also uses a variety of tabular presentations, such as the dotted lines in the 'types of graphic' topic, to give you examples of various layouts. In each of your reports, you should select what you consider to be the optimum presentation, and use it throughout.   3.5c

If graphics make your report clearer, use them - sensibly. If not, don't use them just for the sake of it. And remember that they are not an end in themselves, but merely a tool to emphasise your points.

The Report Report
Notes and Observations

This business expansion plan layout follows the rule of fives - the numbering is grouped into sections and subsections of five or fewer topics.

SECTION / subsection	TOPICS
1 INTRODUCTION	
1.1 Objectives	reasons for presenting plan (codifying own intentions, raising external finance)
1.2 Scope	work done on plan, restrictions on distribution and use
1.3 Executive summary	main financial results and forecasts, benefits of proposed strategy, resources and finance sought
2 BUSINESS	
2.1 History	origins, development of market, products, processes, customer base and current resources and recognition (keep it short)
2.2 Market	overall size and content of current and potential market, characteristics, opportunities, competition, own customer base
2.3 Products and processes	layman's description of products, their benefits to customers, technology, production processes, materials, supply base
2.4 Management	directors, management, staff, professional advisors, banks and other associates, management and financial control systems
2.5 Equipment and resources	buildings, fixed and moveable equipment, factory and office facilities, technology, production systems
3 POTENTIAL	
3.1 Strategy	key opportunities and threats in market, proposals to address them, marketing and product needs and supporting resources
3.2 Positioning	strengths and weaknesses of company, and where it is at present in relation to strategic objectives
3.3 Action plan	specific initiatives, resources, costs, timing, management of plan, risks and their mitigation
3.4 Financial forecast	summary of projections, showing returns on products and areas, effects on security, risk levels, other key factors
4 STRUCTURE	
4.1 Corporate structure	group and company structure, legal aspects, trading agreements, other limiting or enabling factors
4.2 Financial structure	shareholders, lenders, leasing, inter-company arrangements, guarantees, other obligations
4.3 Organisational structure	group and subsidiary companies, joint ventures and other partnerships, management structures down to appropriate level
APPENDICES	
A Detailed financial results	last three years' results in management format (statutory accounts presented separately with report)
B Detailed financial projections	detailed budget for next year, outline budgets for two further years, sensitivity analysis
C Product brochures	bound into report if of manageable size, otherwise presented separately
D Summary of assets	list of main fixed assets, major stock and work in progress categories, major receivables with ageing summary

THE REPORT REPORT
3. LAYOUT
3A EXAMPLE OF REPORT NUMBERING - BUSINESS EXPANSION PLAN   App 3A

The Report Report
Notes and Observations

The following contents headings appeared in a company's standard contract of employment, resulting in a document which although only two pages long was somewhat daunting to a new employee.

FIRST PAGE	SECOND PAGE
TITLE	ACCOUNTABILITY
START DATE	DUTIES
LOCATION	TRAINING
RESPONSIBILITIES	MANAGEMENT
REPORTING	SAFETY
NOTICE	COMPANY RULES AND PROCEDURES
REMUNERATION	STANDARD OF WORK
WORKING HOURS	BEHAVIOUR
OVERTIME	GRIEVANCE
LEAVE ENTITLEMENT	PENSION
TRAVEL	CONFIDENTIALITY
SICK LEAVE	DESIGN RIGHTS
APPRAISAL	

Not only were there 25 section headings to wrestle with, but they were not in any logical sequence or grouping. For example, responsibilities were separated from duties (did anybody know the difference?) and pension was nowhere near remuneration. The contract was rearranged as follows:

FIRST PAGE (operational relationship)

1. Position
- 1.1 Title
- 1.2 Start date
- 1.3 Location
- 1.4 Reporting
- 1.5 Responsibilities
- 1.6 Appraisal

2. Commitment
- 2.1 Employment aim
- 2.2 Working hours
- 2.3 Safety
- 2.4 General rules
- 2.5 Training

SECOND PAGE (personal expectations)

3. Conduct
- 3.1 Standard of work
- 3.2 Behaviour
- 3.3 Grievances
- 3.4 Confidentiality
- 3.5 Design rights

4. Entitlement
- 4.1 Remuneration
- 4.2 Overtime
- 4.3 Pension
- 4.4 Travel
- 4.5 Leave
- 4.6 Sick leave
- 4.7 Notice

The employee now has a much more understandable document. The logic of the groupings is:

- section 1 - this is what the job is
- section 2 - this is the level of commitment on both sides
- section 3 - this is the standard expected
- section 4 - this is how you are rewarded for doing the above

As a matter of psychology, the entitlement section is placed at the end, so that the employee is more likely to read through the demands being made of him first, and cannot complain about 'the small print at the end'.

The Report Report
Notes and Observations

This report was written under the same principles as those of a 50-page report. However, the objectives, scope etc are absorbed in the title and the text to keep the report on one page. It was used as a marketing document by the author, who sometimes presented it with his CV and a covering letter.

THE TRUE COST OF AN ACQUISITION - how an integration director can minimise it

1. What is the true cost of an acquisition?

Every acquisitive group is well aware that the price paid for an acquisition is only part of the overall cost. As well as the cash/share cost of the deal there is the cost of the planning, the executive time, the professional advice, the due diligence process, the PR, the post-acquisition restructuring, product harmonising and other well-known factors. But there is another major factor which is all too often ignored: the immediate subsequent performance of the management of the acquired company and its effect on profit and cash.

2. What happens to a company after its acquisition by new owners?

Uncertainty, delay, confusion, frustration, disillusionment and even anger are common amongst the acquired management team and their staff. It is bad enough if the company has already been part of a group, but if it has been an owner-managed company the sudden change is even more traumatic in management terms:

a) final authorities rest suddenly with a distant and unknown office from which approval is needed for many matters (capex, contracts, customer credit etc) which were previously decided locally, informally and quickly;

b) tried, tested and fully-understood procedures and principles are subordinated, replaced or dispensed with;

c) familiar and reassuring reports are replaced by unfamiliar ones, with the quantity and frequency of reporting normally increasing considerably without local understanding of its purpose;

d) accounts have to be prepared for many dates and periods (company year-end, acquisition date, group year-end, previous twelve months, and possibly tax dates) in several formats (local statutory, tax and management formats and group statutory and management formats) and considerable additional accounting work distracts the company finance team from current commercial and technical issues;

e) the company suddenly has a much greater weight of forecasting, targeting and reforecasting;

f) management and staff seldom receive adequate explanation for what is (or is not) happening and why;

g) legal issues, public relations, documentation changes and other changes add to the local burden;

h) the management eye comes off the ball, the company begins to drift and morale nose-dives;

i) the entrepreneur(s) if still in the business begin to question the wisdom of the acquisition, and with their stake realised, they rapidly lose the very hunger, ambition and drive which made them an attractive acquisition.

These factors soon result in increasingly serious loss of performance and focus within the company. In addition to deteriorating profits and cash flow, the new owners suffer the cost of redressing the situation:

j) assigning already hard-pressed group executives to work with the dispirited company management team;

k) negotiating costly termination packages for disaffected directors and managers;

l) recruitment of new senior personnel and integration thereof into the company and group;

m) rebuilding morale and trust amongst the subordinate staff;

n) rebuilding customer confidence and recovering lost market share.

3. How can this be cost-effectively prevented?

Assigning an integration director to the acquired company for the immediate post-acquisition period (the length of which will vary with the complexity and character of the situation) will greatly reduce the difficulties. She/he will:

a) work as a member of the board of the acquired company from the day of acquisition;

b) explain WHY the various group procedures and instructions are laid down and what the benefits are, and ensure that the management team (not the integration director) follow them and drive them through;

c) raise the maturity level of the company board and its degree of identification with the group as a whole;

d) ensure that the group for its part gives the company strong direction and support;

e) keep the group constantly apprised of the company's progress and potential opportunities and hurdles.

4. What are the essential qualities of the integration director?

In short, experience, authority and maturity - this is no task for a fresh-faced tyro. The integration director must be well-versed in working at board level within a group, and also of working in a catalytic capacity to develop local management so that they solve their own organisational and commercial problems. Such experience, applied sensitively, firmly and constructively by the right person, will eliminate much of the pain and cost described above.

The Report Report
Notes and Observations

When you have a narrative which covers a number of points, each with a number of consistent elements, consider presenting the narrative in a table. This highlights the relationships amongst the points and their elements and gives you the advantages of graphics and narrative combined.

DEMO COMPANY LIMITED - REVIEW OF WEB SITE

Observation	Implication	Recommendation
The home page takes on average 70 seconds to download	Visitors to the site will lose interest rapidly and many will move to another site before the home page is downloaded	Remove the complex background, the revolving logo and the photograph of the head office from the home page, to enable a more rapid download
The links to and from the home page to the other pages are categorised by type of product	Until the customers have seen the specifications for each product, they will not know which product to select, and may leave the site in frustration	Arrange the links on the home page by customer type, so that visitors can go straight to the types of products which will suit their specific needs.
Of the 23 links to other sites, 5 were not operational	Visitors will rapidly lose faith in the integrity and effectiveness of the site, and may not be converted into customers - even existing customers may go elsewhere	Test all links at least monthly and ensure that any non-operational ones are reconnected
The section on the history of the company gives the dates of introduction of each product	Visitors will realise how old the current product is, and are less likely to order one	Reword the history section to emphasise the age and strength of the company but not the age of its products
The specifications of products marks 2 and 5 are not the same as those shown in the marketing brochures	Visitors are receiving misleading information from the web site or the brochures, or both	Appoint a member of the marketing department to coordinate all product literature and synchronise the updating thereof
The company receptionist was not aware of the web site address when telephoned, and took some time to find it	Visitors will be given the impression of a company which is not ready to do business on the internet and they may turn elsewhere	Ensure that all employees who deal with outside parties are as familiar with the web site address and details as they are with its postal and telefax details

It is readily apparent from the above that you can use a very economical form of narrative in this tabular format and put considerably more information on a page than you can with normal prose. Moreover, you can easily understand the relationships amongst the points. For example, you can see from a glance at the 'implication' column that all of the faults with the company's web site are faults that will tend to keep visitors away and thereby deny business.

THE REPORT REPORT   (note heading at BOTTOM of page in landscape layout)
3. LAYOUT

3D EXAMPLE OF TABULATED NARRATIVE

The Report Report
Notes and Observations

There are hundreds of combinations of lines, shading, colours and font types, sizes, bold and italic which can be used in presenting figures. The Report Report does not recommend colours or shading which tend to obscure text and figures, and which lose quality on being copied or faxed. It recommends a simple, well-spaced style with a minimum of lines.

Demo Company Limited SALES FORECAST - UK£M	Prior year actual 2003-04		Actual Q1	F'cast Q2	F'cast Q3	F'cast Q4	Forecast 2004-05		Change		Comments
Year ended 31 March 200X	Mar-04	Mix	Jun-04	Sep-04	Dec-04	Mar-05	Mar-05	Mix	Value	Mix	
Manufactured products	45.2	67%	11.9	12.4	15.7	9.8	49.8	68%	4.6	1%	*For ease of reading, place comments*
Bought-in products	15.8	24%	4.2	3.7	4.4	3.0	15.3	21%	(0.5)	-3%	*and percentages beside the figures to*
Repairs and services	6.1	9%	1.7	1.9	2.1	2.3	8.0	11%	1.9	2%	*which they refer.*
UK Sales	**67.1**	**100%**	**17.8**	**18.0**	**22.2**	**15.1**	**73.1**	**100%**	**6.0**		
Seasonality			*24%*	*25%*	*30%*	*21%*					*Comment on following items:*
Manufactured products	88.2	55%	22.3	27.0	37.1	29.5	115.9	68%	27.7	13%	*assumptions underlying figures*
Bought-in products	26.0	39%	6.1	4.9	5.5	4.2	20.7	28%	(5.3)	-11%	*methods of calculation*
Repairs and services	3.8	6%	0.7	0.7	0.8	0.8	3.0	4%	(0.8)	-2%	*major trends*
Export sales	**118.0**	**100%**	**29.1**	**32.6**	**43.4**	**34.5**	**139.6**	**100%**	**21.6**		*exceptions to major trends*
Seasonality			*21%*	*23%*	*31%*	*25%*					
Manufactured products	133.4	23%	34.2	39.4	52.8	39.3	165.7	36%	32.3	13%	*Give reference numbers for*
Bought-in products	41.8	62%	10.3	8.6	9.9	7.2	36.0	49%	(5.8)	-13%	*detailed analysis*
Repairs and services	9.9	15%	2.4	2.6	2.9	3.1	11.0	15%	1.1	0%	
TOTAL SALES	**185.1**	**100%**	**46.9**	**50.6**	**65.6**	**49.6**	**212.7**	**100%**	**27.6**		*Align comments on the right*
Seasonality			*22%*	*24%*	*31%*	*23%*					*to give the page a neat appearance*

THE REPORT REPORT
3. LAYOUT
3E EXAMPLE OF TABULATED NARRATIVE

The layout uses the following simple conventions:
a Narrative headings are aligned on the left, so that the eye runs easily down them
b The heading of the report (sales forecast) is more prominent than the name of the company if it is an internal report - for an external report, the reverse may be needed
c Headings for individual columns of figures are aligned on the **right**, so that they are in line with the figures below - if aligned to the left, they will be nearer the previous column
d There are spaces between the columns, so that one can read downwards as easily as one can from left to right
e Bold figures are used for vertical totals and subtotals and the main horizontal total, and negative figures are shown in brackets
f Vertical subtotals are lightly underlined, and vertical totals heavily underlined (less fussy than double-underlining)
g The main units of UK£million are noted in the main heading - all other units (percentages in this case) are annotated and printed in italics to differentiate them
h Accuracy of UK£0.1million has been chosen to give sufficient comparison for the smaller figures, while not showing unnecessary detail in the larger figures

The Report Report
Notes and Observations

3F PRESENTATION OF FIGURES - DIVIDING LINES

*Many report writers, particularly financial ones, have a passion for printing dividing lines between rows and columns of figures. This is probably a subconscious effort to make reports look more technical, and therefore more impressive. The opposite is the result. The whole purpose of dividing lines is to differentiate rows and columns, and so **the more lines you use, the less differentiation you get**.*

For example, in this table everything is boxed and therefore nothing stands out from the rest.

Accidents	Apr	May	Jun	Jul	Aug	Sep	Oct	Nov	Dec	Jan	Feb	Mar	Total
Category A	88	54	48	43	50	61	64	78	125	88	72	70	841
Category B	5	5	1	3	0	4	4	5	9	7	4	7	54
Category C	18	15	16	12	12	21	24	19	31	26	22	25	241
Total	111	74	65	58	62	86	92	102	165	121	98	102	1,136

Now see how it looks when only the quarters and vertical totals are marked with lines.

Accidents	Apr	May	Jun	Jul	Aug	Sep	Oct	Nov	Dec	Jan	Feb	Mar	Total
Category A	88	54	48	43	50	61	64	78	125	88	72	70	841
Category B	5	5	1	3	0	4	4	5	9	7	4	7	54
Category C	18	15	16	12	12	21	24	19	31	26	22	25	241
Total	111	74	65	58	62	86	92	102	165	121	98	102	1,136

The division into quarters gives some shape to the year and makes it easier to find your way and spot the trends. The bigger the table, the bigger the advantage of this second approach will be.

Now consider the general table below. Instead of boxing every item as shown on the left, rule them off every five rows as shown on the right. You can read the table (and count the items) more easily.

Test centres	A	B	C	Total
Bradley	22	1	13	36
Caballe	16	3	9	28
Carr	4	0	7	11
Clare	3	2	9	14
Clayton	0	4	4	8
Evans	0	4	4	8
Hamilton	13	5	15	33
Harper	6	1	3	10
Hibbert	9	4	14	27
Hodgkiss	11	0	0	11
Moon	21	0	2	23
Nock	8	0	6	14
Pilkington	18	7	11	36
Planas	7	3	8	18
Roberts	5	4	4	13
Rouquet	10	4	5	19
Spencer	23	3	12	38
Staples	6	1	7	14
Taylor	17	5	1	23
Van Der Blom	20	1	3	24
Wright	8	2	3	13

Test centres	A	B	C	Total
Bradley	22	1	13	36
Caballe	3	3	10	16
Carr	16	3	9	28
Clare	4	0	7	11
Clayton	3	2	9	14
Evans	0	4	4	8
Hamilton	13	5	15	33
Harper	6	1	3	10
Hibbert	9	4	14	27
Hodgkiss	11	0	0	11
Moon	21	0	2	23
Nock	8	0	6	14
Pilkington	18	7	11	36
Planas	7	3	8	18
Roberts	5	4	4	13
Rouquet	10	4	5	19
Spencer	23	3	12	38
Staples	6	1	7	14
Taylor	17	5	1	23
Van Der Blom	20	1	3	24
Wright	8	2	3	13

The Report Report
Notes and Observations

This imaginative and psychologically effective report was devised by a Machiavellian group financial director for the directors of his subsidiary companies.

*Note that conditional formatting shows **actual** period headings in **bold** text*
Note also that dividing lines are only drawn every quarter, for ease of reading

PROFIT FORECAST - YEAR ENDED 30 JUNE 2003
Actual results to end of period   4   Oct-02

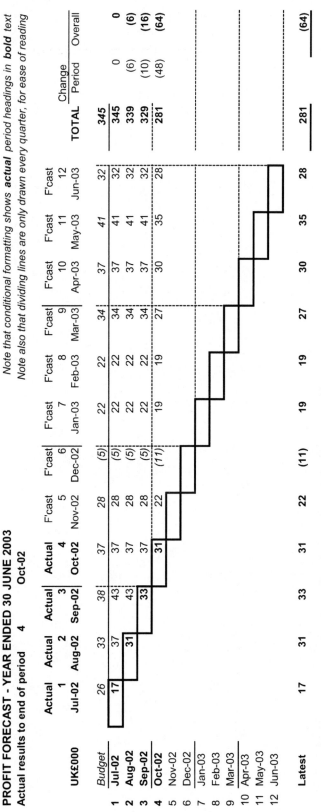

UK£000	**Actual** 1 **Jul-02**	**Actual** 2 **Aug-02**	**Actual** 3 **Sep-02**	**Actual** 4 **Oct-02**	F'cast 5 Nov-02	F'cast 6 Dec-02	F'cast 7 Jan-03	F'cast 8 Feb-03	F'cast 9 Mar-03	F'cast 10 Apr-03	F'cast 11 May-03	F'cast 12 Jun-03	TOTAL	Change Period	Change Overall
Budget	26	33	38	37	28	(5)	22	22	34	37	41	32	**345**		
1 Jul-02	17	37	43	37	28	(5)	22	22	34	37	41	32	345	0	0
2 Aug-02		31	43	37	28	(5)	22	22	34	37	41	32	339	(6)	(6)
3 Sep-02			33	37	28	(5)	22	22	34	37	41	32	329	(10)	(16)
4 Oct-02				31	22	(11)	19	19	27	30	35	28	281	(48)	(64)
5 Nov-02															
6 Dec-02															
7 Jan-03															
8 Feb-03															
9 Mar-03															
10 Apr-03															
11 May-03															
12 Jun-03															
Latest	17	31	33	31	22	(11)	19	19	27	30	35	28	281		(64)

a   The subsidiary company director enters his budget for the year along the first row (the use of brackets to denote a negative figure is an international convention).

b   At the end of month 1 (July in this case) he enters the actual result in the bold-outlined box, and reforecasts the remainder of the year along the rest of the row.

c   He has not reached his budgeted profit for month 1, so he has increased his forecast for months 2 and 3 to get back on track by the end of the first quarter.

d   In month 2 he again fails to reach his budget, and this time does not assume that he can make up the lost ground - the column at the right shows slippage of 6.

e   He falls short again in month 3, but holds to his budget for the rest of the year - the slippage of 10 for the period brings him down to 16 below budget overall.

f   With a shortfall in month 4, he recognises that he is consistently not reaching budget and reforecasts the remainder of the year downwards - slippage of 64.

g   The group financial director receiving the updates of this report each month can see how each company is faring and how well the local directors are forecasting.

h   Optimistic budgets followed by downward-spiralling forecasts are an all-too-common feature of group subsidiaries - this format highlights it for remedial action.

THE REPORT REPORT
3. LAYOUT
3G PRESENTATION OF FIGURES - IMAGINATIVE EXAMPLE (cascade format)

App 3G

The Report Report
Notes and Observations

The pie-chart below came from the corporate brochure of a high-technology company selling equipment to highly qualified people. Did those people really need a pie-chart to illustrate a 70-30 split in sales?

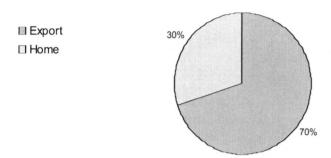

A much more effective use of a pie chart was by a regional council explaining to its council tax payers how the region's taxes were spent. Many of the tax payers would not be highly numerate, but they could easily see which types of expenditure absorbed the most and least funds. A good graphic.

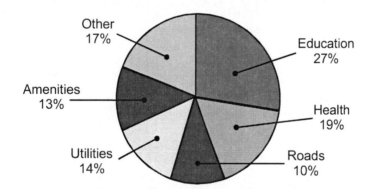

Probably the most misleading graphic in common use is the isometric (tilted) pie chart, in which the perspective can distort the various 'slices' of the pie. Note how the 25% slice occupies much more of the page area than the 30% slice.

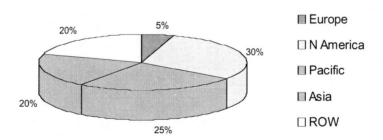

Think before deciding to use a graphic!

The Report Report
Notes and Observations

Line graphs are a general-purpose technique for showing how one or more items vary in relation to another in a progressive situation (usually from one period of time to the next). They are at their most effective when all the items being compared are similar and use the same units of measure. For example, below is a comparison of sales volumes of similar three products over four periods of time:

Sales Volumes (tonnes)

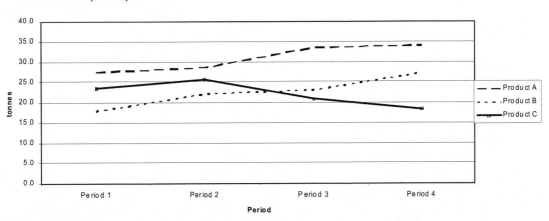

A line graph assumes that quantities progress evenly from one point on the graph to the next, which is not always the case. For example, a graph of scores in a rugby match should show the score remaining constant between points, then rising vertically in a step to the new level when further points are scored.

Where the items being compared have more complex relationships, or do not easily fit on the same vertical axis, you may well be better to present them in a table instead, and show relative percentages to emphasis the relationships. Consider this review of aircraft losses over four periods:

BOMBER ATTRITION	Period 1	Period 2	Period 3	Period 4
Sorties flown	864	919	1,058	1,266
Increase in period		6.4%	14.9%	19.9%
Aborted - tech failure	38	48	67	94
Abort rate	4.4%	5.2%	6.3%	7.4%
Failed to return	72	104	101	103
Loss rate	8.3%	11.3%	9.6%	8.1%
Mission completed	754	767	888	1,069
Completion rate	87.3%	83.5%	84.1%	84.5%

The numbers of sorties flown and missions completed are much greater than the other numbers, making it difficult to present them on the same graph (this would normally be achieved by having two scales on the vertical axis). But the most important aspect of the figures is the percentages, which themselves could be shown on a graph.

However, it is more effective overall to view the figures and percentages together in a table. From this we can see that the increasing level of activity is causing a higher percentage of aborted missions from technical failures. But we do not know how many of the failures to return result also from technical failures and how many from enemy action, but given that technical failures are likely to increase from wear and tear, defensive measures appear to be reducing the rate of shoot-downs after their initial surge. We also do not know how many of the aircraft which aborted were later able to continue operating, and how many which returned were too badly damaged to fly again. Not a case for a graph!

The Report Report
Notes and Observations

A bar graph performs almost the same function as a line graph. It shows the changes in a group of characteristics over several sectors. For example, consider the following review of accidents in four areas:

Casualties by area

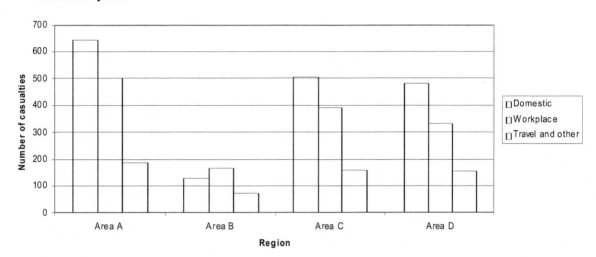

Note that the graph shows fairly clearly the changes in the mix in each area, and the differences in overall numbers. But if instead the separate areas were consecutive periods of the same area, the graph would not show the trend through the periods as well as a line graph would (App 3I).

Some people have difficulty in distinguishing colours, and many faxes and photocopiers do not reproduce colour. Your graphics should therefore achieve their clarity from the way in which they are laid out, not by using colour. However, the boxes opposite 'Domestic' etc in the key on the right are too small to indicate clearly which pattern is which. This is a typical example of badly-designed software, as the boxes cannot be increased in size.

It is readily apparent from the above that the bar chart gives an immediate visual impression of the relative sizes of the figures concerned. It is therefore a powerful tool for oral presentations, in which the audience usually has less time to assimilate the information than do the readers of a written report.

However, in an ongoing management situation, such as monthly management meetings, it is important to consider the psychology of presenting information in graph form. If you present a set of graphs to a management team the day before a meeting, they will arrive at the meeting knowing the broad relationships amongst the figures you have charted, but they are unlikely to have considered the figures in any greater depth (ie they will not have quantified these broad relationships, and quantifying them is normally an essential part of understanding them). It may seem strange, but you may have made the report too easy for them.

If you only present them with a table of values and percentages, they will have to study the figures and understand the relationships in detail (ie the relative rates of increase and decrease in the items you are comparing) to be able to perform at the meeting. The graphs will be welcomed more by the team, but the tables may well create a better meeting. One could argue about this for a long time!

One thing is almost certain. If you give the team graphs for one meeting, you will be stuck with them - the team will want them for every meeting.

The Report Report
Notes and Observations

Stacked bar charts are popular for showing how different components making up a total vary from period to period or area to area. However, they are usually a good example of the eye being given information which it cannot quantify or compare in detail.

Murders

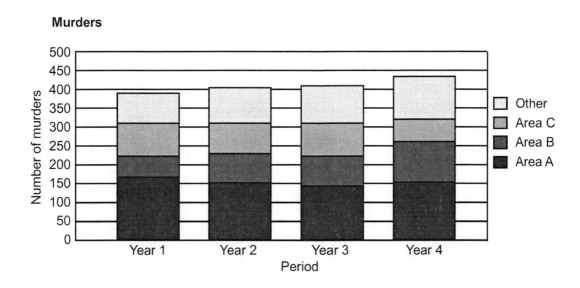

It is difficult to compare for instance area B from year to year, because the sections are not level with each other, and they are being measured against different totals. Moreover, for all but area A, you have to subtract the bottom of the range from the top to give you the size of the range, and that is only roughly. All the graph gives you is an approximate view of the changes in mix and overall levels.

In this case, it is much more effective simply to present the table of figures from which the stacked bar chart was prepared, and insert percentages showing the mix in each year and the increase from year to year in each area. To any numerate person, 'a decrease of 9% in area C from year 1 to year 2' means much more than the third block in the second column seeming to be a bit smaller than the same block in the first column.

Murders	Year 1		Year 2			Year 3			Year 4		
	No	Mix	Inc	No	Mix	Inc	No	Mix	Inc	No	Mix
Area A	164	43%	-9%	149	38%	-7%	138	34%	8%	149	34%
Area B	62	16%	39%	86	21%	10%	95	23%	14%	108	25%
Area C	81	21%	-9%	74	18%	-4%	71	17%	-8%	65	15%
Other	78	20%	21%	94	23%	14%	107	26%	6%	113	26%
Total	**385**	**100%**	**5%**	**403**	**100%**	**2%**	**411**	**100%**	**6%**	**435**	**100%**

In the table, you can read along the rows or down the columns, and the inclusion of percentages allows you to compare both the overall sizes of the sectors and their relative importance within their countries. Remember that statistics are all about comparison, so unless your graph enhances comparison along with quantification, it is probably a waste of your time and the addressees' time.

The Report Report
Notes and Observations

3L EFFECTIVE OR NOT? - GANTT CHARTS

The Gantt chart, developed by the US management consultant Henry Gantt, is deservedly popular for planning projects and monitoring their progress against the plan. Below is a simple example, in which the shaded areas indicate the progress of the project.

Xerxes product launch - timetable

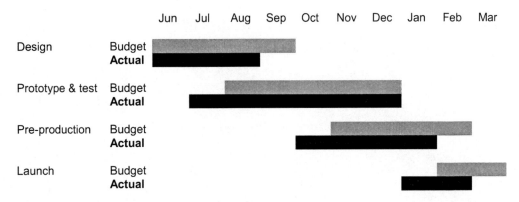

Reporters generally use different shadings, symbols or colours as above to show different features of the various parts of the project. This normally involves using special project management software.

However, you can present a much more effective Gantt chart simply by using a spreadsheet, and adding numbers to denote the application of man-days, tonnages, costs or any quantities you want. This makes the Gantt chart a powerful management tool as well as a reporting tool.

Xerxes product launch - man-days

		Jun	Jul	Aug	Sep	Oct	Nov	Dec	Jan	Feb
Design	*Budget*	7	8	12	14					
	Actual	8	19	16						
Prototype & test	*Budget*			3	14	6	8	11		
	Actual		4	13	7	2	16	3		
Pre-production	*Budget*						6	16	21	23
	Actual					10	10	31	36	
Launch	*Budget*									15
	Actual								19	13
Total	Budget	7	8	15	28	6	14	27	21	38

The story of this project is clear from the spreadsheet. The company applied additional personnel to the project, to launch the product a month early, but at a 15% overrun on man-days. You can format the spreadsheet conditionally to shade each cell if the value in it is not equal to zero.

The Report Report
Notes and Observations

When discussing statistics relating to a geographical area, the use of a simple map can be helpful.
- *It gives an indication of the spread of the area and the distances involved.*
- *Where the divisions of the area are arbitrary (areas assigned for sales or other responsibilities often do not follow legal boundaries) it clarifies them.*

The statistics relating to the area can be shown in a table accompanying the map, or on the map itself as in the example below.

If the map is in a written report, it can be quite detailed, but if it is being presented to an audience in slide format, it must be kept simple. Even the map below would probably be too detailed for a slide, as the print is relatively small. If you are giving the different areas separate colours, ensure that they are light colours, as dark backgrounds make the print difficult to read, especially on a slide.

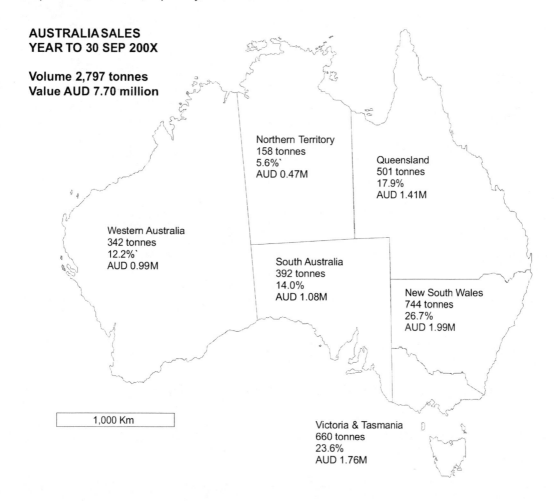

**AUSTRALIA SALES
YEAR TO 30 SEP 200X**

**Volume 2,797 tonnes
Value AUD 7.70 million**

Northern Territory
158 tonnes
5.6%`
AUD 0.47M

Queensland
501 tonnes
17.9%
AUD 1.41M

Western Australia
342 tonnes
12.2%`
AUD 0.99M

South Australia
392 tonnes
14.0%
AUD 1.08M

New South Wales
744 tonnes
26.7%
AUD 1.99M

1,000 Km

Victoria & Tasmania
660 tonnes
23.6%
AUD 1.76M

As the map does not state what is being sold, it is presumably an internal document. The statistics would be more useful if they included the percentage of sales value (as well as of volume) and the net margin on the sales in each area. AUD is the international abbreviation for Australian dollars.

Note that the percentage for South Australia is stated as 14.0% and not 14%. This is for two reasons:
- to maintain a consistent presentation - all the other areas are displayed to 0.1%
- to make it clear that it is not an error (eg 14.7%, with the decimal omitted in error).

The Report Report
Notes and Observations

The process flow chart below on the left shows the sequence of processes in a metal foundry and machining operation. The table on the right records the weight of metal which is used, scrapped, recycled and produced from 1,000 Kg of input. The combined use of a chart and tabulated figures explains how the processes are sequenced, and how much they produce. This is intelligent use of graphics and statistics together. It was all prepared on a spreadsheet, to use the calculation facility.

SCRAP LOSSES IN METAL FOUNDRY AND MACHINING OPERATIONS

Percentages are measured against the original input of 100%

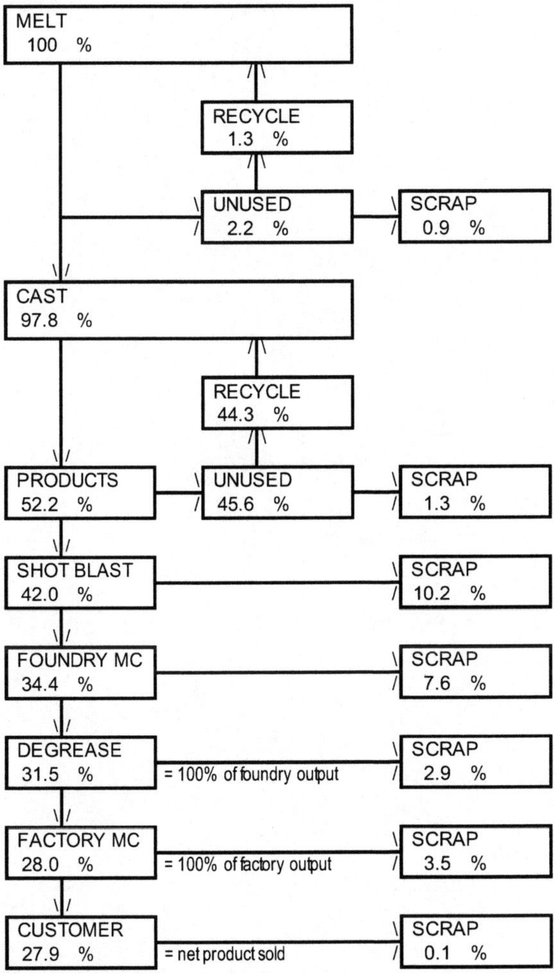

WEIGHT in Kg (negatives in brackets)

	Input	Scrap	Product
Material weight	**1,000**		
Melt recycle	(13)		
Melt process scrap		(9)	
Cast recycle	(443)		
Cast process		(13)	
Degrease inspection		(102)	
Machining process			
Finishing process		(29)	
Stores inspection		(35)	
Customer inspection		(1)	

Flow chart (left column):

- MELT 100 %
- RECYCLE 1.3 %
- UNUSED 2.2 % → SCRAP 0.9 %
- CAST 97.8 %
- RECYCLE 44.3 %
- PRODUCTS 52.2 % — UNUSED 45.6 % → SCRAP 1.3 %
- SHOT BLAST 42.0 % → SCRAP 10.2 %
- FOUNDRY MC 34.4 % → SCRAP 7.6 %
- DEGREASE 31.5 % = 100% of foundry output → SCRAP 2.9 %
- FACTORY MC 28.0 % = 100% of factory output → SCRAP 3.5 %
- CUSTOMER 27.9 % = net product sold → SCRAP 0.1 %

Although 1,000Kg of metal is input originally,
456 Kg is recycled later, and only 544 Kg is actually used.
Of this, 189 Kg is scrapped, leaving 355 Kg of product,
which is an output of 65.3% on the net weight of material used.

Working that in reverse, if you need 1,000 Kg of product
you will incur 532 Kg of scrap
and require 1,532 of material net of recycled material recovered.
This will require a gross input of 2,816 Kg before recycling.

	Input	Scrap	Product
Net material usage	**544**		
Scrap		(189)	
PRODUCT CONTENT	65.3%		**355**
Product weight	65.3%		**1,000**
Scrap		532	
Net material needed	**1,532**		
Gross input needed	**2,816**		

The Report Report
Notes and Observations

There are few situations or problems which cannot be described in a two-dimensional format. Setting out a situation in a simple matrix or similar schematic helps both the writer and the reader gain a clear understanding of the situation. The only limit to this technique is your vision of the circumstances.

Real life: *a group holding company had three operating subsidiaries, of which A and B manufactured products, and C was a distributor. The three subsidiaries, all struggling, operated independently in most respects, but certain functions were carried out centrally by the holding company to achieve economies of scale. These central functions were purchasing, delivery, engineering, administration and finance. Such a split of activities tended to cause confusion with regard to managerial responsibilities, so the group presented to the managers at all levels a simple table which they easily understood.*

GROUP RESPONSIBILITIES

Category	Company A	Company B	Company C	Group
Sales	Sales Managers	Sales Managers	Sales Managers	
Materials price				Purchasing Mgr
Materials usage	Production Mgr	Production Mgr	Stock Controller	
Labour costs	Production Mgr	Production Mgr		
Marketing	Marketing Mgr	Marketing Mgr	Marketing Mgr	
Selling / support	Sales Managers	Sales Managers	Sales Managers	
Distribution				Transport Mgr
Development				R & D Manager
Admin				Group Controller
Factory				Works Engineer
Finance				Group Controller
Operating profit	Managing Director	Managing Director	Managing Director	Group Man Dir
Inventory	Stock Controller	Stock Controller	Stock Controller	
Receivables	Sales Managers	Sales Managers	Sales Managers	
Payables				Purchasing Mgr
Working capital	Managing Director	Managing Director	Managing Director	Group Man Dir

You cannot get much simpler than that - clear and robust. A few practical points:
1. By referring to job titles instead of names, the chart was not affected by staff changes.
2. Each manager was targeted on the areas for which he was responsible, which were also those over which he had control. His pay was related to the performance in those areas.
3. Delivery costs are normally a direct cost of sales, but because the group operated a weekly national delivery schedule, the cost was relatively fixed, and was therefore treated as an overhead.
4. It may surprise some readers to see the company managing directors and the group managing director at the bottom of the chart, but their main responsibility was the bottom line, not the top line.
5. Did it work in practice? Yes - the group achieved remarkable quality, profit, and cash flow results.

The Report Report
Notes and Observations

The Report Report
Notes and Observations

Having worked out what you are going to include in your report and how you are going to lay it out, you now have to think about what narrative style you should use. As always, you have to start by thinking about the addressees. What style are they going to find the most digestible and acceptable?

SUMMARY   Ref

Your reporting style should take full account of the environment in which the addressees operate. Whether you wish to blend with style of this environment or to counterbalance it or be critical of it, you have to understand it. The main aspects of the addressee environment are:

- **the overall and individual cultures, and the sensitivities attached to them (you may have to dig**   4.1b
  deep in the organisation to establish whether the culture professed by the addressees genuinely   4.1c
  exists - the louder they trumpet about their progressive culture, the less likely you are to find it)   4.1d
- **the status of your addressees and their consequent priorities and concerns**   4.1e
- **the specific political background to the report (possibly special circumstances)**   4.1f/g
- **the subject matter**
- **receptiveness or otherwise to humour or challenges**

a) **Objective**   Ref

The objective of a reporting style is to convey information in the manner in which the readers will be able to assimilate it most easily and without annoyance.

You should therefore use the style to which the addressees will be most receptive, to the extent that it is suitable for your subject. It is not necessarily the style which they themselves would use, since they may not be skilful reporters, or they may report at a different level. If the addressees have a variety of cultures, the report should be in a universal style appropriate to them all. However, it may be necessary to tailor it to suit the most important addressees while still making it assimilable by the rest.

You therefore need to have a clear understanding of the addressee environment, and to be prepared to ascertain a 'middle path' in narrative style if the addressees have widely differing cultures and expectations, as do the readers of this report.

b) **Culture and related difficulties**   Ref

Before writing your report, ensure that you understand the culture of your individual addressees. It may dictate elements of the reporting style you adopt. If you do not consider culture to be important, then pause to reflect that more people have been killed because of cultural differences than for all other non-natural reasons combined.

Firstly, there may be various forms of address or reference which you should either use or avoid. In the modern western world these are relatively few, but check carefully in the case of nationalities and cultures different to your own. Broadly, the further east you travel from the Greenwich meridian, the more acute are the cultural sensitivities. To some extent, the reverse happens when you travel west. The informal culture of North America is becoming increasingly common in the UK and the rest of western Europe, but it is by no means universal in these parts.

cont'd

The Report Report
Notes and Observations

b) Culture and related difficulties (continued)   **Ref**

Secondly, you need to consider the characteristics of the individual addressees themselves. Are they formal, conservative, highly political, cost-conscious, image-conscious, secretive, defensive, relaxed, dogmatic, pragmatic, obsessed with detail or what? An otherwise well-constructed report can have a poor impact simply because it is at odds with the culture of the addressees. The smaller the organisation, the more its culture will ape that of its leader. Conversely the larger an organisation is, the more you will find pockets of different cultures, sometimes fiercely guarded. Be alert.   2.3d

During your information-gathering, have a look at relevant internal reporting used by the addressees' organisation. Some organisations have distinctive styles of internal reporting, and you can replicate their style to some extent, unless it is alien to your own natural style or unsuitable for the subject of your report. The organisation may also have a consistent format of layout, which may be appropriate for you to use, to give the addressees a feeling of instant familiarity with your report. On the other hand, people do not always like the style used in their own organisation and are looking for something refreshingly different. Find out.

You may also have the chance to review reports submitted by your competitors, and to gauge your addressees' reactions to them. You can gain bonus points by avoiding any pitfalls in your competitors' reports.

Asking people about their culture is an unreliable process. Leaders of organisations are usually reasonably honest about their organisational and technical shortcomings (more tactfully   2.2b
referred to as 'areas needing improvement') but for some reason they normally avoid speaking   2.3d
clearly and straightforwardly about their culture.

Indeed, a form of reverse honesty applies. The leaders who genuinely practise what the culture clichés preach can be recognised by the fact that they stress the areas in which they have not fully upheld their principles. As they are genuinely trying to run the kind of effective and ethical organisation described in the clichés, they have real concerns about areas of shortfall, and genuinely welcome advice. But the ones who say glibly 'we are committed to quality' or 'this is a people business' are less likely to confront the real underlying issues and can often be uncomfortable in these areas.

Despite the reservations expressed above, you still have to consult with the leaders on the cultural issues, but then you must move rapidly down through the organisation and verify whether or not their alleged culture really exists in practical - repeat, practical - terms. What   2.3d
really happens amongst customers, suppliers and staff, and why? And if you find any unsatisfactory issues which you need to bring back to the leaders for further discussion, you must do so sympathetically, to help them to admit the problems and discuss them openly.

At the back of this section is list of cultures commonly found in organisations or parts of   App
organisations. Study these and learn to recognise them, and others like them.   4A

When considering an organisation's cultures in your reporting, first ask yourself whether or not a culture you are encountering has a negative effect on the aspects on which you are reporting. If there is no appreciable negative effect, than you probably have no need to concern yourself with the culture (you may even wish to praise it in your report). If, however, the culture appears to have a direct adverse effect on your subject, you must consider two issues:

cont'd

The Report Report
Notes and Observations

b) Culture and related difficulties (continued)   Ref

- the adverse effect of the culture on the performance of the organisation
- the way in which the culture will distort the information provided to you

Firstly, if you consider that the culture lowers the organisation's performance in an area which matters to your report, you will have to prove that this is so. Even if you interview both sides of a cultural divide and attempt to express your opinion fairly, whichever side you criticise more will automatically reject your findings and claim bias on your part. You must therefore provide written evidence to support your opinion. This evidence should satisfy the following conditions:

- it should as far as possible be generated or accredited by, a part of the organisation which is not subject to the cultural problem and which is therefore unbiased
- it should be numerical (eg reject rates, delivery dates etc) rather than subjective
- it must cover the established trend, and not merely reflect isolated incidents.

Secondly, if you are gathering information in an area blighted with an adverse culture, you must take a similar approach or you will obtain information which is biased and may well rank as misinformation (not intended) or even disinformation (deliberate):

- always, repeat *always*, obtain corresponding information from both sides of the cultural divide, and also from persons who are independent but close enough to have a reliable appreciation of the problem
- use numerical information as far as possible
- use information which is part of a consistent flow, not an isolated exception.

When reliable information which you have collected shows a different picture from that which your interviewees have presented to you, it is normally best to discuss the information tactfully with the interviewees as soon as possible. Your discussion may lead to further revelations and require further information-gathering and further discussion. This is normally safer than delaying presenting them with a conflicting picture in your completed report, only to find that there are other circumstances of which you have not been made aware.

The discussion approach should always centre tactfully around facts. For example, 'These supply dates show a lower failure rate than you suspected; is there some other factor I should be considering here?' will broach the subject without actually impugning the accuracy or integrity of your interviewee. If his complaint about the supply source is merely based on prejudice against the group supply operation, he will not be able to disprove your findings, but he will have time to reconsider his position.

More difficult to gather is the non-numerical type of evidence, but the approach is broadly similar. For instance, if a department complains about receiving inadequate instructions, you must obtain copies of the instructions received and sent (always investigate both sides of the cultural divide) to obtain a true picture of the effectiveness of the instructions. You will also have to check the routing of the instructions; they may have been correctly issued but not received owing to a problem which is not the fault of either party.

To sum up, you must pay attention to the general overall culture of any organisation on which or to which you are reporting, and to any specific cultures which exist in different parts of the organisation. You must then take an impartial approach to determining the reality underlying any difficulties arising from these cultures, and use factual (preferably numerical) evidence to arrive at supportable statements in your report.

The Report Report
Notes and Observations

c) Status

You must understand the status of your addressees before you start writing. If their own perception of their status is higher than the reality, be particularly careful.

For example, if your report attributes blame for some unsatisfactory circumstances, it will have to be sensitively worded, but without diluting the truth, if the addressees carry responsibility for those circumstances. And take special care also when contradicting the views of the addressees in your report.

Similarly, if you are making recommendations, it should be clear whether these are to be implemented directly by the addressees or by persons under their authority. Advising the chief engineer that he must clean the repair shop is not tactful, but he is responsible for ensuring that one of his subordinates does.

Finally, do not be like the major consultancy firm which habitually began its reports with the word 'Gentlemen' - even when some of the addressees were female.

d) Sensitivities

What is the political background to your report and its addressees? For example, the following reporting environments have their own typical political considerations:

▪ academic, medical or scientific	highly particular about their territory
▪ legal or financial	generally risk-conscious
▪ security-related	specifically risk-conscious
▪ market-related	sceptical, waiting to be convinced by you
▪ disciplinary	defensive, proof-oriented, seeking impartiality

The tone of a report, even to the same addressees, could vary greatly according to the subject and political background. A report promoting a course of action such as a marketing initiative may have to be upbeat or persuasive, while one covering an investigation into an alleged wrongdoing should be serious. A report on a dispute or a set of options must be seen to be scrupulously impartial and unemotional.

Ensure that you understand the political climate before starting your narrative. You also have to decide whether it is appropriate for your report to blend with the politics or to swim deliberately against the tide. If it is the latter you will need to be doubly careful, particularly in respect of your choice of words.

e) Subject matter

In some cases it may be advisable to adapt your reporting style to counterbalance the subject matter instead of empathising with it.

For example, a proposal for finance for a traditional business such as metalworking may lack appeal to prospective providers of finance, simply because such industries tend to be (somewhat unfairly) regarded by finance professionals as unexciting. You can mitigate this with a more upbeat style than normal for such a proposal, with the credible use of words such as 'rapid response' and 'flexibility' to emphasise that the business, although traditional, is to be dynamically managed. But do not use overstatement.

Ref (c) Status

App 4G

1.1a

Ref (d) Sensitivities

4.1c

4.1e

4.3h

4.3

Ref (e) Subject matter

4.2c/ d

cont'd

The Report Report
Notes and Observations

e) Subject matter (continued)

Ref

Conversely, a proposal for a high-technology company may suffer from the intangible, fast-changing, high-risk nature of the product, which can make potential investors apprehensive. A more sober approach than normal would be appropriate here, using words such as 'proven', 'solid' and 'controlled' to reassure potential backers that the risks have been reliably assessed and will be contained by responsible management, and the ultimate goals and related rewards are be likely to be achieved.

f) Humour

Ref

Be most careful. One person's humour is another person's bad taste.

Life in general and business in particular are taken too seriously. But it is one thing adding some humour to a meeting of people whose faces and reactions you can see and judge, and quite another trying to be funny in cold print.

The secret as always is understatement. If your humour is expressed in mild terms which have the reader wondering if it is intended or not, you have probably pitched it at the right level. But beware of howlers, especially accidental puns.

4.4b

Real life: A farmer received a legal letter complaining about his livestock continually breaking bounds and damaging his neighbour's property. He responded through his solicitors with the excuse that on buying the farm some years back he had had to deal with very poor fencing, which he was still repairing. The neighbour's riposte to the farmer's solicitors included the words: 'I have some sympathy regarding your client's problem with his fences, but it is customary to secure one's enclosures before introducing livestock, not after.'

The comment could be interpreted:

- as a straightforward statement
- as gentle humour
- as withering sarcasm.

The invasions of livestock ceased.

g) Provocative writing

Ref

How challenging or provocative should you be in your narrative style?

Real life: A specialist wrote a management manual for a group of many companies, some of whose managers could charitably be described as traditional in their outlook. The first draft of the manual challenged many of the group's accepted practices. The client received the draft with approval, but many of their managers complained that the style was provocative. The specialist replied that since the whole purpose of the manual was to provoke people into thinking laterally and acting to improve their performance, there was no point in writing it in any style other than a provocative one.

3.2e

A compromise in style was eventually agreed. The more progressive managers in the group wondered what all the fuss was about, while the diehards still protested loudly at being jolted out of their comfort zones. Coincidentally, the division with most of the diehards was sold shortly afterwards, and the group's performance improved notably.

cont'd

The Report Report
Notes and Observations

g) Provocative writing (continued)   Ref

This illustrates two problems:

- the question of mixed culture levels, discussed earlier
- the question of how adventurous a report-writer should be.   4.1b

Since most of this subsection warns of the dangers of offending readers' sensibilities, we need to redress the balance a little. Your reports are intended to make the readers think and the need to be sensitive does not mean that you have to be bland in your reporting. You are reporting from a degree of knowledge and authority, and if you see the need for improvement, it is your responsibility to convey that need in your report.

You must, however, be careful. When you make observations and recommendations which run against the conventional wisdom, you must be sure that you have researched your facts correctly and fully, and that your interpretation of them is tenable. If you are satisfied that you are right and that you are not overstating your case, then by all means be provocative, provided that you keep the tone of your provocation strictly impersonal, and constructive rather than destructive. You only live once, and the clients who are most worth having are the ones who genuinely want to read, hear and face the truth.

In a perfect world, all writing would be provocative.

h) This report   Ref

In choosing a style in which to write *The Report Report*, which is addressed to people of all cultures, the author had to choose between two conflicting parameters:

- the purpose of the report is to teach by example, and it should therefore be written in an impersonal, universal style which could safely be used for a report on any subject

- the report is also intended to serve as a companion and source of reference to report-writers of all kinds, and should therefore be written in an accessible, colloquial style.

After much consideration and two or three false starts, the author decided that setting an example was the main priority. However, he adopted the suggestion of one of the editors to lighten the overall tone by introducing each subsection with a preamble in a less formal style. This style was extended to the real life examples and various comments in the appendices.

Anything written in italics in this report is therefore in a less formal style which you should not adopt unless you are sure of your readership.

The informal preamble and postamble given to each subsection of this report is not a normal   App
reporting practice, except in instructional texts. However, there is no reason why you should not   1A
use this approach, although you will probably have to use a more formal style.

From the above considerations, adopt whatever style will convey your message most tellingly. Remember that having your report read, understood and accepted is not enough; you have to stimulate the addressees to think about what you have written and implement the actions you have recommended. This will usually involve writing in a style empathetic with the addressee environment, but in a few cases, you may have to challenge it, deliberately and carefully. But don't overdo it; these are the people who are paying you, and they have to see your challenge as being constructive.

The Report Report
Notes and Observations

No matter what style you have chosen, you have to report clearly. This section details the practical aspects of clarity which should prevail in every report. Clarity comes from thinking about what you write, how you express it and how the reader will interpret it. It makes perfect sense to you, but ...

SUMMARY

Ref

Clarity of expression is primarily a structural matter. You must structure your narrative so that it is unequivocal, and the following practices are used consistently.

▪ Seek to achieve eloquence (powerful understatement) and avoid loquaciousness (mindless overstatement).	4.2c 4.2d
▪ Avoid unnecessary use of the first person.	4.2e
▪ Use the active mode wherever possible.	4.2f
▪ Choose your tense according to the circumstances and stick to it.	4.2g
▪ Do not shift between singular and plural within the same context.	4.2h
▪ When making conditional statements, use the 'will' mode.	4.2i
▪ Use a consistent narrative style, but vary it when emphasis is needed.	4.2j
▪ Use note format in lists and annotations, but keep it clearly separate from prose.	4.2k
▪ Be consistent in your use of all these elements of your narrative.	4.11

a) Objective

Ref

The objective of clarity is to make yourself readily understandable. No more, no less.

All

b) Simplicity

Ref

Good English is simple English. The same goes for any other language.

In other words, don't say 'at this moment in time'; say 'now'. People who are not comfortable with writing reports or speaking at meetings often resort to an unnaturally formal and stilted choice of words. The result invariably sounds pompous, and has the effect of making the writer or speaker harder to understand, not easier.

App 4B

App 4H

c) Eloquence v loquaciousness

Ref

After a gap of nearly 300 years, the Scottish Parliament was reopened in 1999 by Winifred Ewing at a ceremony in Edinburgh.

She could have rambled on at length about the hopes of a nation, the pent-up expectations, the national identity and culture. In fact, she could have recited the entire litany of clichés which had been churned out ad nauseam by the media over the previous few months. That would have been **loquaciousness**; saying a lot but telling you little.

Instead, she said: 'The Scottish Parliament, adjourned in 1707, is hereby reopened.'

Those stark words captured the entire history and emotion behind the moment. Three hundred years of having the posturings and processes of government peacefully tucked away in another country was about to end for Scotland. That was **eloquence**; saying little, but telling you a lot. Eloquence is a combination of simplicity, brevity and directness.

4.2d

The Report Report
Notes and Observations

d) Understatement

Ref

In the 1960s, overstatement became part of the culture of English-speaking people throughout the world, even of those learning it as a second language. Words like 'fantastic', 'amazing' and 'incredible' which should have strong meanings became used habitually to describe quite mundane items for which they were not intended. These words lost all their emphasis and today when someone calls something 'brilliant' it probably means that it is mildly enjoyable in some unspecified way.

The result of this is that understatement is now the most powerful form of expression. When someone tells you loudly that something is utterly disgraceful, totally unacceptable and an insult to common decency, you ignore him. When someone looks you in the eye and says quietly that it is not acceptable, you listen to him.

App
4G

e) First, second and third persons

The 'persons' are as follows:

- first person   I/me, we/us   my/mine, our/ours
- second person   you   your/yours
- third person   she/her, he/him, it, they/them   her/hers, his, its, their/theirs

Avoid using the first person unnecessarily. People's dislike of listening to someone using 'I' and 'me' often in conversation is well-known, and the same applies to written reporting. Using 'we' is less wearing on the reader than using 'I', but even 'we' can be annoying if used a lot. The reporter should be concentrating on the readers, not on himself, which is why good reporting and business writing seldom use the first person.

4.2 f

There are exceptions, of course. It is common and probably necessary to use the first person where giving:

- an opinion: 'we consider that the outbreak can be contained'
- a commitment: 'I shall ensure that this is checked weekly from now on'
- an account of your actions: 'I had already warned him of this danger'

1.3a

Use the second person freely. The author refers to himself in the third person, but uses the expressions 'your addressees' and 'your report' etc, because this is all about developing your reporting skills. Some reports refer to the addressees in the third person, which gives the report a more formal tone.

f) Active and passive modes (also called active and passive 'voices')

Ref

There are two modes of expressing action:

- active: someone does something
  example: the radio operator receives the message

- passive: something is done (by someone, who is often not mentioned, leaving confusion in the reader's mind as to who does it)
  example: the message is received (by the helmsman? the officer of the watch?)

Always use the active mode if you can. The reasons are:

- it describes the action in its logical sequence - *the virus attacked the cattle*
- it uses a simpler sentence structure
- it ensures that you state who or what carries out the action (especially important when you are giving an instruction or recommendation).

cont'd

The Report Report
Notes and Observations

f) Active and passive modes (continued)

Ref

However, the passive mode can occasionally be useful.

- It enables you to avoid using the first person if you are the subject of the sentence, and do not wish to personalise the statement.

4.2e

- It enables you to avoid a sensitive situation, such as criticism of your addressees - instead of stating 'the commander had not established contact' you can state 'contact had not been established', thereby leaving the addressees or some other party to determine who was responsible for the problem (this approach would be unacceptable if you were specifically tasked with attributing responsibility).

App
4G

When writing reports or issuing instructions, many people subconsciously slip into the passive mode to the point where it becomes a habit. Instructions such as 'The tank will be refilled daily' are a recipe for chaos unless it is clearly stated either immediately before or after that instruction either who is to refill it, or who is to ensure that it is refilled.

Note: this report could freely use the passive, since it consists entirely of instructions to you, the reader. You are therefore the subject throughout. However, this report **uses** the active in most cases. The passive **is used** sparingly.

g) Tenses

Ref

Which tense should you use for reporting? In general you should use the tense which is most logical to what you are describing.

- Use a past tense to describe events which have happened.
- Use a present tense to describe a situation which exists at the date of your report (but this can be dangerous - see below).
- Use a future tense to describe events which are expected to happen.

There are of course several types of each of the three tenses mentioned above, but that is something with which you should already be familiar. In the USA, the perfect and pluperfect tenses are seldom used in conversation; the past historic is the norm. Where a UK English speaker might say 'I have done it already' (perfect tense) or 'I had done it already' (pluperfect tense) depending on the context, a US English speaker will usually say 'I did it already' (past historic) regardless of the context. This is a common example of how US English is an easier conversational language, but less effective when precision is needed.

Do not use the present tense unless you are certain that what you are saying is completely true at the date of your report. For example, if you inspect a structure for damage on 13 September and state in a report dated 20 September that it 'is intact', you are running the risk that it has been damaged in the intervening week. You can cover your position by stating in the 'scope' section that all information was correct at the date of inspection, but it is still safer and more truthful to use the past tense.

1.2

Finance professionals, who are habitually risk-conscious, are surprisingly often guilty of reporting in the present tense on findings which may well have changed between their investigation date and their reporting date. This is possibly because they work to a great extent on their judgement. Engineering and science professionals, who are more strictly driven by facts, tend to use the past tense in reporting findings.

The Report Report
Notes and Observations

h) Singular and plural   Ref

It is easy when writing about something in general terms to keep switching between the singular and plural forms, thereby confusing the readers. In one paragraph you are writing in a 'they [all] are' (plural) form, and in the next you are using 'each [one] is' (singular). Such inconsistency can make your narrative difficult to follow.

Decide which form you want to use and stick to it. Most people tend to use the plural form in conversation, and instinctively use it in writing. However, the singular form usually gives a more precise understanding if you can remember not to stray from it.

Decide whether you are going to treat collective nouns (group, squadron, company, division, board, council, department, platoon etc) as singular or plural, and use that format throughout. Technically they are singular, but tend to be referred to as plural in conversation. If you write 'The Board is unanimous' (singular) do not follow it with 'that the group accept' (plural).

i) Conditional statements   Ref

You may have to write in a conditional tense; that is a mode in which the word 'if' is used. You have two alternatives:

- the 'would' form
- the 'will' form.

Whether you use 'would' or 'will' you have to use other tenses which correspond with whichever mode you are using. For example:

- if you **found** that the aircraft **had** already left, you **would** have to take a train, and you **might** not arrive in time
- if you **find** that the aircraft **has** already left, you **will** have to take a train and you **may** not arrive in time.

People generally use the 'would' mode more often in conversation, and therefore tend instinctively to use it in reporting. However, it has several disadvantages.

- It can lead to more tortuous-sounding language.
- It sounds vague, uncertain, evasive, unauthoritative, grovelling and Dickensian.
- It is favoured by people who use overblown phrases such as 'utterly disgraceful, totally unacceptable and an insult to common decency'.   4.2d
  App
- It can contain an implied negation ('it would...' can be followed by an unspoken 'but...', as   4G
  if there is an underlying expectation that it is not going to happen).

You should therefore use the 'will' form wherever possible. If you **do**, your reporting style **will** be more direct, clear and authoritative.

j) Emphasis   Ref

We have already discussed achieving emphasis by visual means in the layout of your narrative.   3.3h
Much more importantly, you also need to be able to achieve emphasis in your narrative style, and here we have an exception to the principle of consistency. To create emphasis you usually have to break the consistency of your style for the point you are emphasising. And you need to use a variety of ways in which to change your style, to avoid repetition.

cont'd

The Report Report
Notes and Observations

j) Emphasis (continued)   Ref

Examples of changes in style to create emphasis are:

- a very short sentence
- an incomplete sentence (i.e. one without a verb - really a non-sentence, and it must be short - for example: 'No more, no less.')   4.2a
- a sentence beginning with a conjunction (especially 'but')
- a rhetorical question
- a non-rhetorical question which you answer yourself
- repetition - to be used very sparingly
- a short lapse into conversational English (e.g. using 'isn't', 'don't' etc - this is not advisable unless you are sure of your addressees)
- a brief lapse from authority into apparent or real bewilderment ('how that is intended to happen is not clear') - but be careful; this may appear sarcastic
- a diversion into irony or humour, provided that it is used with care.   4.1f

The above variations in style interrupt the flow to the reader and make him think more sharply about what you have written. However, there are a few cautions to bear in mind when emphasising.

- Avoid repeated use of the same technique, as it will rapidly become annoying to the reader (more difficult than you may imagine - instruct your external reviewer to watch out for habits and pet phrases).   5.3h
- Do not use emphasis persistently, or it will cease to be emphatic.
- Do not resort to overstatement for emphasis.   4.2d
- Make sure you know the rules of grammar before you break them deliberately.   4.4a

Mechanical emphasis by underlining, quotation marks, exclamation marks, etc tends to be the hallmark of the younger writer writing to a close confidant or colleague, and suggests a personal relationship, and usually light-heartedness. It can also convey an apologetic tone or a lack of confidence (or so it seems to me!). In a formal report, try as far as possible to achieve emphasis   3.3h by variations in your style rather than by mechanical means.

And if you are resorting to exclamation or question marks in a formal report, do not use multiple ones. They create a very informal mood!!!

k) Note format   Ref

There are occasions when note format, an abbreviated version of normal prose, is acceptable. The most common of these occasions are:

- when giving operating instructions
- when annotating a chart, diagram or picture
- when presenting a list.

Note format usually excludes 'a' and 'the' and any non-essential words and punctuation, and is   3.3d acceptable in the contexts listed above. However, you must ensure that you do not drift between   4.4d full prose and note format within the same context. This results in sentences such as 'Suspect was found by occupant in the subway with the stolen items in carrier bag', and does not read well.

Note format is often used for minutes of informal meetings, and for headings and lists, in which   SA2- formal language can be tedious to read.   B

The Report Report
Notes and Observations

l) Abbreviations   Ref

Many reports would be difficult to write well without using abbreviations. Constant repetition of long phrases or measurements would take up space and make tedious reading. And tabulation of figures would be cumbersome if one had to write 'four thousand Singapore dollars' instead of the number '4' in a column headed 'SGD000'.

Abbreviations therefore have an important function in making a report easier to read. But they will only make it easier if they are themselves clearly understood. To ensure this, you should:

- use internationally recognised abbreviations where they exist, unless they could be confused with other abbreviations
- if no recognised abbreviations are available, explain your abbreviations, in the same way as   1.4a
  you give definitions of other terms used in your report.

Some abbreviations have more than one meaning, and there is therefore scope for confusion. For example, 'M' or 'm' usually means a million times, but 'm' numerically means one thousandth and to confuse matters further it is also the standard abbreviation for metres and miles. 'M' can also be used to mean a thousand times. So you may even have to explain standard abbreviations, to let readers know which standard ones you are using.

When dealing with currencies, the abbreviation should include the country as well as the currency unit. Francs, marks, rials, pesos, rupees, dollars, pounds and some other units are each used by several countries, so the country name is essential. There are standard three-letter codes used by bankers and treasurers for all countries; some examples are USD (US dollar), CHF (Swiss franc), ZAR (South African rand) and, illogically, GBP (UK pound). US$ and UK£ are both unmistakable, and are often used in preference.

m) Consistency   Ref

We have discussed above the benefits of varying your reporting style to achieve emphasis. However, these variations must be exceptional. The readers want a flow of consistent expression which carries them comfortably through the report.   4.2 j

In particular, the structural elements of your report must remain consistent, as they provide the framework on which the reader comes to rely. These elements include:

- technical terms, including abbreviations   1.4a
- numbering, dating and layout   3.2
- persons, modes, tenses as described above   4.2
- other conventions you have adopted for the report   1.4b

Clarity is a combination of simplicity, consistency and correctness, with only an occasional deliberate deviation for emphasis. It requires you to think all the time about your words and how you put them together.

Probably the most complimentary word to describe a reporting style is 'crisp'. If someone describes your reporting as 'crisp', you can feel justifiably proud of your work.

The Report Report
Notes and Observations

In the previous subsection we discussed the need for simple structural clarity. But structure is not the only component of a readable narrative; you have to use appropriate words within the structure. Below are some simple guidelines for choosing your words, or at least for avoiding unsuitable ones. The appendices to this section give examples of common misuses which you should avoid.

SUMMARY   Ref

With carefully-chosen precise wording you can express yourself powerfully. The more you use it when speaking, the less time you will have to spend thinking about it when writing. But if you do not take care with the words you use, your reports will be unclear and inaccurate, and confusing and irritating to the readers.

The pitfalls which you should avoid are:

- use of jargon, except where it is used and expected by your addressees   4.3b
- use of clichés, which make you sound as if you have no mind of your own   4.3c
- use of quotations, which do the same, and are often irrelevant anyway   4.3d
- use of obscure words, except where they are unavoidable   4.3e
- use of incorrect expressions - consult a dictionary for every new word you hear, to learn what it really means, which may not be what people use it to mean   4.3f
- foreign expressions - unless they will be readily understood by your addressees   4.3g
- emotive words - express everything in factual, impersonal terms   4.3h
- extreme words - you will find yourself overstating regularly and being unconvincing   4.3i
- expressions which have different meanings in other geographical areas   4.3j/o
- colloquial phrases using familiar small words out of context   4.3k
- non-specific words - instead of saying 'good' say what is good about it   4.3l
- misstatements of fact - boiling the kettle instead of the water in the kettle   4.3m
- padding - words which pad out your narrative and add nothing to it .   4.3n

That is a long list of misuses to avoid, and there are others. The positive way to do it is to concentrate on writing simple, crisp narrative. It is better to have to add the occasional complex expression in your review than to have to simplify a host of them.   5.3

a) Objective   Ref

Appropriate wording is essential to achieving:

- clarity   4.2
- accuracy   2.4
- authority   4.1
- sensitivity   4.1
- readability

Incorrect or inappropriate wording on the other hand can cause:

- confusion
- misinformation (the reader is not confused, but accepts inaccuracy as fact)
- annoyance, possibly to the point of offence
- loss of your credibility

Assimilating the 'right' words comes only with practice. But in this section we can accelerate the process by identifying categories of 'wrong' words.

The Report Report
Notes and Observations

b) Jargon

Ref

Every area of work or interest has its own technical terms, and these terms are necessary to enable people within that field to discuss clearly its technicalities. If you are reporting to addressees who are themselves in the field on which you are reporting, then you should use the technical terms of that field, as they will be understood and expected by the addressees.

However, when technical terms are used outside their field, they become jargon. The deliberate use of jargon is a tactic of insecure people, trying to hide behind a knowledge that others do not have. It can also be a form of showing off, another notable habit of insecure people. The most popular form of jargon is abbreviation to initials, especially where the initials form an acronym (i.e. an existing word, such as PLUTO - Pipeline Under The Ocean)

It may, however, be necessary to use unfamiliar terms simply because they are either the only terms or the best terms to describe what you are reporting upon. If your terms are likely to be unfamiliar to any of your addressees, you should include a glossary of the terms at the front of your report, or spell it out on the first usage if it is in one section only. Otherwise, use widely-recognised terms as far as possible.

1.4a

c) Clichés

Ref

A cliché is a word or phrase which is overused to the point where it has lost its impact and sometimes even its very meaning. Most clichés are instigated by broadcasters or journalists coining expressions which are copied by their less imaginative counterparts and thereafter taken up by the public, often out of context. Most professions have their own clichés as well as the ones used by the general public.

For example, the words 'significant' and 'totally' became very common in professional English in the 1980s, and are usually misused. Some clichés are nonsensical, such as 'abundantly clear'; abundance relates to quantity, and clarity to quality.

App
4C

The most common occurrence of clichés is in CVs (curricula vitae, or résumés). Anyone recruiting for a junior-to-middle-management position is inundated with résumés from people claiming to be hands-on, highly-motivated, commercially-oriented, results-focused, pro-active self-starters with good interpersonal skills. Meaningless waffle - pass all of these CVs to your personnel manager for a polite rejection.

Instead, hire someone who writes something original, such as: 'I get results by breaking big problems down into their components, which I delegate to appropriate people. This gives me time to direct and encourage them and make sure that the work is done on time and on budget.' There you have a manager who thinks for himself and deals with reality.

When a word or phrase is in frequent current use, exclude it from your vocabulary. By avoiding overused words and choosing your own expressions you will:

- **think** about what you are saying instead of grabbing the nearest convenient buzz-phrase, which may not be exactly what you are trying to express
- distinguish yourself from the majority of your competitors by having your own analysis of matters, rather than regurgitating everyone else's
- improve the quality of your reporting by using a refreshingly unaffected style which does not ride on some current bandwagon.

The Report Report
Notes and Observations

d) Quotations

Quotations fall into the same bracket as clichés. They are someone else's words, so avoid them and use your own. In fact they are worse than clichés because people often fail to find a quotation appropriate to their context and are left quoting (or misquoting) something of dubious relevance. Moreover, the fact that a remark was made by somebody famous does not automatically mean that the remark was sensible. Two examples, from people in a position to have known better:

- Neville Chamberlain, September 1938: *'I believe it is peace for our time'*
  Result: the biggest war in history

- Ronald Reagan, the 1980s: *[Colonel Ghaddafi of Libya is]* *'the mad dog of the Middle East'*
  Fact: Libya is in North Africa - not even in the Near East, let alone the Middle East

If you trawl through a dictionary of quotations, you will find another problem, namely that most quotations are mundane, even dull. Apart from Churchill's legendary insults and Andy Warhol's prediction of the increasingly fleeting nature of fame, the most notable quote of the twentieth century came from Mandy Rice-Davies, whose fame did not arise from her literary prowess. *'He would, wouldn't he?'* gained immortality for immorality and ended forever the notion of automatic respectability for people in high places.

If you are desperate to use a quotation, you are welcome to this one concocted by the author to exempt himself from having to make any: *'He who quotes a lot probably hasn't an original thought in his head.'*

Ref

App
4G

e) Obscure words

If an obscure word is either the only word or emphatically the best word to convey your meaning, then use it. If that is the right word, the readers will have to learn it.

Otherwise, avoid using it. It annoys a busy reader to have to look up words or simply not understand them (few offices have a comprehensive dictionary to hand). Worse, it may make the readers take an instinctive dislike to you as someone who likes to parade his intellect. As a report writer, you should have a dictionary and thesaurus, and should use them to ensure you select suitable words.

Remember that a word which is common to you may be unknown to the readers.

Ref

f) Incorrect expressions

Language evolves by two main processes:

- people create new words (e.g. connectivity, infomediary, swimathon), particularly in technical environments
- people misuse words, the misuse becomes generally accepted and the word either changes its meaning or acquires a new meaning in addition to the original one (for example, the word 'nice' once meant over-particular, or foolish, but is used now as a vague expression of approval)

The difficulty arises when a word is in the transitional stage. At what point does a word become misused to the extent where the misuse becomes a correct use? You cannot assume that common usage is correct usage, so develop the habit of looking up a word in a reliable dictionary when you first hear it. At the end of this section is a list of words commonly misused; there are very more than are listed.

Ref

App
4I

App
4B

cont'd

The Report Report
Notes and Observations

f) Incorrect expressions (continued)   Ref

If you consider that your skill with words needs improving, concentrate on reading well-written newspapers, magazines, reports and books. Daily newspapers sometimes suffer from being written against tight deadlines, but the more responsible British dailies and some Commonwealth dailies manage to sustain a high standard of English. Magazines drawing from erudite contributors probably contain the highest quality of writing.

If you do not have time to read, listen to non-pop radio in preference to watching television (radio   4.3c
is a better medium for this because it relies almost entirely on words). You will develop an ability to recognise effective language and expression, and will begin to absorb it. Remember to filter out the clichés, which you will soon recognise.

For the second time in this report, the subject of names arises. Get them right. Do not refer to   2.4 i
North Africa as the Middle East, nor British as English, nor Slovaks as Czechs. Do not refer to Ireland as Southern Ireland. Do not put 'The' before Ukraine, Lebanon, Algarve, Gambia or Crimea. Do not spell Bewlay as Bewley. A high percentage of incorrect expressions involve incorrect names, indicating sloppiness and ignorance.

g) Foreign expressions   Ref

Foreign expressions (usually Latin, French or German, but also Nordic, Spanish, Russian, Arabic and many others) fall into two categories:

- those which have no direct or convenient equivalent in the English language
- those which are merely foreign equivalents of English expressions.

Where a foreign expression has no direct equivalent in English, it is usually accepted as an English word, even if it is spelled and pronounced as in its original language. Examples of this are 'ad hoc' (Latin), 'restaurant' (French), 'zeitgeist' (German), 'glasnost' (Russian), 'siesta' (Spanish), 'robot' (Czech) and musical terms, which are Italian. European languages increasingly use each other's words, and some words like 'visa', 'hotel' and 'taxi' are almost universal.

Foreign words, if still regarded as foreign, are generally written in italics, and retain their accents. Once they become fully accepted as English words, they cease to be written in italics, and often lose their accents. Hence 'rôle' is usually written as 'role'. However, it may be advisable to retain accents to show differences in pronunciation, as in the case of 'résumé', which would otherwise be pronounced as 'resume'. Accents can cause problems, as modern software and keyboards are sometimes not able to produce them. 'Reykjavík' and 'naïf', for example, defeat some software packages.

Where a foreign expression has a direct English equivalent, ask yourself:

- Does using the foreign term enhance the point you are making?
- Are the readers likely to recognise it and understand it?

If the answer to both of those questions is yes, then use the foreign expression. If not, use the English equivalent.

In general, be careful. It is easy to assume that a foreign term is widely recognised, but it may not be. For example, Latin terms such as 'inter alia' and 'pro tem' are in everyday use in business circles in Scotland, but less so in England and only rarely in the USA. The UK and USA are more insular with languages than mainland Europe.

h) Emotive words   Ref

Be careful of words which may be emotive in the minds of the readers. This is easier said than done, as a word may be quite innocuous to you, but may be interpreted quite differently by a reader. This is yet another example of why you must always put yourself in the reader's position while you are writing.

For example, in the appendix listing various types of report, there is the comment 'David is a   App
popular name'. The first draft of this report stated 'David is a common name', which was correct   1A
within the context. But 'common' can also be used as a derogatory term meaning ill-bred or
undistinguished, and could be interpreted that way by any reader called David. Since that is not
the author's intended meaning, he replaced the word 'common' with the word 'popular' (used
even by kings and saints!).

It is just as easy in writing as it is in conversation to offend with an innocently intended word or   5.3h
phrase. Moreover, since you know what you meant when you wrote it, you can easily miss it
when reviewing your work. It is therefore important that your work is reviewed by someone else
who is alert to such misinterpretations.

Avoid making blanket criticisms unless they are of a strictly technical nature, and supported by
hard evidence. For instance, if you condemn open-plan offices in general, you can bet that one
of your senior addressees is a keen advocate of them, and you may humiliate him in front of the
others. If you need to make that point, write: 'Separate enclosed offices would be the most
suitable for this operation because ...' You will have made your point specifically, with reasons,
without even mentioning open-plan offices, let alone making any blanket condemnation of them.
People may disagree with your point, but they cannot reasonably take offence.

Finally, do not admit in your reporting to having any emotions or sensitivities of your own.
When giving an opinion, do not say 'we feel that'; say 'we consider that'. Feeling suggests an
emotional reaction, but considering indicates the outcome of a logical thought process. If you
wish to express annoyance, frustration or any negative reaction of your own, avoid using the first
person, and express the circumstance in unemotional words such as 'unacceptable',   4.2e
'inappropriate', 'unsatisfactory', 'unsuitable' or 'untenable' and give reasons, to show that it is a
practical dislike rather than an emotional one.

This confirms that you are a stable and impartial reporter who makes strictly rational
judgements, not personal ones. There is nothing wrong with having strong feelings, but you may
put yourself in an indefensible position if you express them in a report.

i) Extreme words   Ref

Avoid embellishing adjectives with adverbs which indicate an extreme or even high degree of a   4.2d
condition. Common examples are:

very	highly	greatly	totally	much [more, less etc]
significantly	seriously	deeply	utterly	many [more, fewer etc]

They create the effect of overstatement, which we have already discussed. When reviewing your   4.2d
report you may have to delete a number of these words, as they are common in conversation and   5.3g
therefore easy to use instinctively in writing. The result is that you can find yourself writing in   4.2d
overkill, which has the same wearing effect on the reader as listening to someone talking too
loudly and emotionally. It also deprives you of an extra gear when you really do want to state
something emphatically.

The Report Report
Notes and Observations

j) Words which do not travel well

Ref

Remember, especially when writing in English, that words can change their meaning when used in different areas. The most obvious example is the difference between US and UK English. US English is steadily gaining dominance in the world, even in the UK, and has the advantage that it is simpler, but the disadvantage of lacking many of the subtleties and nuances of UK English. Some of the differences are not even particularly subtle; spoken US English hardly recognises the perfect and pluperfect tenses, and rarely distinguishes between adjectives and adverbs.

In the USA 'the aircraft will be airborne momentarily' means that the plane will take off very soon. In the UK it means that it will stay in the air for only a few seconds. A dyke is a ditch in England, but the opposite (a wall) in Scotland. In some parts of the UK you can need an interpreter within 100 kilometres of your birthplace.

Similarly, the terms 'Five Nations' and 'Six Nations' refer in Europe to a rugby union tournament which began with five countries and was expanded to six. In North America the same two terms refer to a confederation of Sioux peoples, the confederation having similarly increased from five to six participants.

Unless you are closely familiar with the different usage of language in areas where your report may be read, stick as far as possible to mainstream English, with as few slang or esoteric terms as possible. Use a reviewer familiar with the other usages.

5.3h

k) Familiar words used out of context

Ref

You should also avoid if possible using conversational expressions involving common small words followed by prepositions which take them out of context. Examples are:

- put up with
- dead set
- go off
- fed up.

Such phrases cause difficulty to people reading English as a second language, and sometimes also to English speakers from a different region, because:

- the common words almost invariably have a different meaning from their normal ones (someone who is 'dead set' on something is certainly not dead, and someone can be 'fed up' because he has not been fed)
- the use of prepositions varies considerably from one language to another, and from region to region within the same language
- some of the phrases are hard to distinguish from similar phrases with quite different meanings ('put up' and 'put up with' in the UK have different meanings, and 'put up' in the USA - as in 'put up or shut up' - means something else again)
- the phrases can cause difficulty in choosing and understanding the order of the words, a situation 'up with which it is difficult to put'.

Instead of such phrases, use the specific words available. For example:

- put up with   tolerate, suffer, endure
- dead set   determined, adamant, immoveable, inflexible
- go off   depart, decompose, explode, stop, stop liking, become derailed
- fed up   irritated, frustrated, disgruntled, annoyed, bored

The Report Report
Notes and Observations

l) Non-specific words

Ref

General words such as 'good' and 'bad' are of little value in reporting, because they do not specify the characteristics which make something good or bad. The whole point of reporting is to communicate specific facts and ideas and you must therefore use specific words to say exactly what is good or bad about the topic.

So instead of telling your colleagues that this report you are reading is 'good', tell them that it is clear, easy to read, instructive, thought-provoking and full of useful suggestions. Tell them that it is relevant to all kinds of reporting and essential to anyone whose work involves writing reports, or to anyone who is dissatisfied with receiving illogically-structured and confusingly-worded (not just 'poor') reports from his subordinates, and who needs them to improve their skills.

4.3k

m) Mis-statements of fact

Ref

Always describe exactly what the facts are. So that this becomes instinctive, cultivate the habit of doing it in conversation. For example, do not say 'boil the kettle'; say 'boil the water' (you do not want molten metal). In this instance, you are not using incorrect words, you are using correct words incorrectly, which has a similar effect.

4.3 f

This will not sound pedantic, provided that you do not try and correct other people's terminology. It will, however, help you describe situations precisely.

Real life: A diver inspecting a subsea structure reported that 'most of the bolts are loose'. The client sent out a boat with expensive spare bolts, pneumatic impact wrenches and more divers, only to find that the bolts were secure, but some lock-nuts were loose and could have been tightened manually. The remedial expenditure had been unnecessary and the client was not amused.

n) Padding

Ref

If you review your work carefully you will find a number of unnecessary words which you use as 'padding'. Such words are intended, usually subconsciously, to make the words sound and flow better, but they seldom do. You should therefore remove them.

App 4D

App 4E

Editing out padding is a laborious task, so you are better to purge it from your everyday speech so that economy of expression becomes a habit. Examples of spoken padding are:

- obviously - if it's obvious, why say it?
- to be quite honest with you - aren't you always honest?
- sort of - used frequently by people of all levels of education almost to addiction - the author has heard 'we sort of went and sort of sat down and sort of talked'
- you know - often used several times in each sentence
- combinations of the above - 'sort of style type thing, you know' is often heard

There are also less colloquial fillers, some of which are repetitive and others merely unnecessary. There are so many possibilities with these that there is no convenient catch-all description of them. Some examples are therefore included at the back of this section, to give you some idea of what to guard against. A common type of padding is tautology, in which an expression includes two or more words with the same meaning, such as 'it follows therefore', of which the author had to edit several from his drafts.

App 4D

App 4E

The Report Report
Notes and Observations

o) Insular expressions   Ref

Some words keep their meaning when they travel, and yet still cause difficulty. For instance, words such as 'overseas' and 'foreign' do not change their meaning, but you should not use them in an international context.

Real life: *a group holding company instructed its subsidiary companies to provide details of 'overseas tax' in a section of a report. Subsidiaries in other countries quite properly included any UK tax they suffered in 'overseas tax', because the UK is overseas from where they were situated (landlocked countries were a little confused by the term). The holding company should have used the term 'non-UK tax', which is unambiguous. Fortunately, someone spotted the anomaly before it was too late.*

Place names are not safe, either. For example, there are Londons all over the world, an Aberdeen in Hong Kong, several Newcastles in the UK alone, and Garfields and Springfields dotted all about the USA, so you may have to state which one you mean. As always, consider how your addressees will interpret your words.

p) US or UK spelling?   Ref

It does not normally matter whether you use US or UK spelling, unless there is a specific requirement (e.g. legal) for one or the other. Whichever one you use, stay with it for the entire report, and make sure that your word-processing software does the same. Much of the software used in the UK will default to US spelling unless you set it to UK spelling.

Warning: do not Briticise or Americanise place-names. Greensboro, Harrisburg and Pittsburgh (USA), and Scarborough, Middlesbrough and Dunstanburgh (England) should always be spelt as shown, and Long Beach Harbor should not be changed to Long Beach Harbour.

And note that although most British people spell '-ise' and '-isation' with an 's', the preferred spelling per reputable British dictionaries is '-ize' and '-ization', just as it is in the USA. Your word processor may default to the 'z' spelling even under UK settings. Note, though, that even under the '-ize' convention, there are a number of words such as 'advertise' and 'supervise' which still have the '-ise' ending. If you use the '-ise' ending throughout, this will not cause you a problem.

The secret with wording, as it is with any aspect of style, is to concentrate on writing simple matter-of-fact English. Don't use conversational expressions, but don't use pompous or pretentious wording either. And always consider your readers - how will they interpret what you've written?

The Report Report
Notes and Observations

Teaching grammar is beyond the scope of this report. Anyone who is writing reports should long since have mastered the basics of the language in which he is reporting. However, it has not escaped the author's attention that some people reach quite dizzy heights of journalism, company directorship, political leadership and other communication-intensive fields without displaying much knowledge of how to string together a correct and meaningful sentence. It would probably be unfair to criticise them for this, as they may well have risen to their position as a result of other technical skills, and had to develop their communication skills relatively late in life. Nevertheless, grammatical errors in a high-profile situation can result in the speaker or writer becoming a figure of derision instead of one of authority.

> *If your grammar skills are not as high as your other professional skills, you have four choices:*
> - *go back and study it, through either a textbook or classes (by far the best option)*
> - *get someone else to write your reports (easier said than done, and it doesn't solve the problem)*
> - *get a secretary skilful enough to correct your grammar (not as easy as it may seem)*
> - *concentrate on work which does not involve writing reports (probably a backward step).*

The best use we can make of this subsection of the report is to consider the worst common mistakes, which centre around sentence structure and punctuation. If you can avoid these, any remaining errors should be less important.

SUMMARY   Ref

Even if you do have a good grasp of the fundamentals, there is still plenty of scope for you to make errors. Most of these will involve the structure of your sentences, which if not carefully assembled will leave the reader unclear as to which parts refer to which other parts. To avoid such confusion:

- before you write each sentence, think about what you intend to convey   4.1b
- identify the main clause of your sentence   4.1b
- arrange the subordinate parts of the sentence (if there are any) so that they relate clearly to the main clause   4.1b
- consider what punctuation is needed, and ensure when you have inserted it that it gives the meaning you intended for it   4.1d

a) Objective   Ref

The purpose of grammar is to present your chosen words (provided that they are the right words) in a format which is clear and unambiguous.   4.3

Grammar is ignored to a large extent in conversation, because speech occurs in the context of a dialogue, and is supplemented by tone of voice, facial expressions and gestures. Moreover, people in conversation can confirm their understanding at any point with a query. In conversation, many sentences are left unfinished, because it has already become apparent that the message has been conveyed.

Written communication has no such responsive help. The whole purpose of writing down your thoughts is that someone can read and understand them without the benefit of the aforementioned expressions and gestures, and without the opportunity to question you.

What grammar does is establish a set of rules regarding the use of words. Some English grammar comprises subtle rules of detail which ideally should be understood and followed, but which in practice can be ignored without too much damage. However, the structural rules which we consider here are essential.

The Report Report
Notes and Observations

b) Sentence construction

Ref

Sentences are constructed in sections. As a rule, each section relates to the section nearest to it. Therefore you have to arrange each sentence so that the various parts of the sentence are next to the bits to which they are intended to refer. If the sentence does not come with the parts in the right order, it is a simple matter to rearrange it.

Real life: *consider these gaffes from the morning news:*

The missing oarswoman's rowing boat was sighted by a Liberian tanker with no signs of life aboard. Whilst Liberian tankers have been known to be somewhat sparsely crewed on occasion, it is likely that the news scriptwriter was trying to say that it was the rowing boat which showed no signs of life. The script should have been: *A Liberian tanker sighted the missing oarswoman's boat with no signs of life aboard.* (Note how much easier it is to get it right by using the active instead of the passive mode).

4.2 f

The boy's body was found by a climber huddled in a ditch. This indicates that the climber was huddled in a ditch. What was meant was: *A climber found the boy's body huddled in a ditch.* Again, the use of the passive mode creates the problem.

4.2 f

There is a conference on suicides in Edinburgh today. The sentence suggests that suicides are taking place in Edinburgh today, and there is a conference (at an unspecified place and time) to discuss them. It should read: *In Edinburgh today there is a conference on suicides.*

The Royal Navy today ran up the Union Jack on an island in the South Atlantic which had been taken down by the Argentines. This clearly states that the Argentines had taken down the South Atlantic. If you removed 'in the South Atlantic' it would state that the Argentines had taken down an island. What the writer meant was: *On an island in the South Atlantic, the Royal Navy today hoisted the Union Jack, which had taken down by the Argentines.* Note also that although the expression 'ran up' is a correct term, it could create visions of some unfortunate matelots scrambling up a flagpole, so 'hoisted' would have been better, being unambiguous.

4.3k

The Prime Minister is speaking to Parliament on cracking down on the European drug trade today. Does that mean that the pushers and dealers can get back to business as usual tomorrow? Hardly. The word 'today' should have been placed after the word Parliament or at the beginning of the sentence.

below

And so it goes on, day after day. When we hear that *a man broke into a house armed with a machete,* we must assume that a man armed with a machete broke into a house. And one of our editors has contributed an airline favourite: *take the lifejacket from under your seat and place it over your head.* Difficult, indeed.

Such gaffes are mildly amusing in the course of everyday life. They are potentially serious when a factually critical sentence is misconstructed to give entirely the wrong meaning. Construct your sentences carefully and then read them over.

What the news scriptwriters do wrong (whether through time pressure or inexperience we do not know) is to put the main clause (i.e. the headline) at the beginning of the sentence and then add two or three related phrases, so that it is not clear which phrase refers to which other phrase. This also happens instinctively in conversation.

cont'd

b) Sentence construction (continued)   Ref

Usually, it is structurally easier to put the main clause in the middle of the sentence, and the related phrases on either side of it, so that they are both next to the main clause and cannot refer to any other part of the sentence. This takes a little forethought, as you will often find that your fingers have typed the main clause before you have thought about the related phrases. Consider the whole sentence before you start writing, and remember to use the active mode in most cases.

A brief digression: the use of the phrase 'cracking down' (above) was possibly one of that particular radio station's well-known deliberate puns, but in a serious report such ambiguity may have to be edited out. Accidental puns are easy to make, and not just by sports commentators.   4.1 f
In a marketing report on a comb manufacturer the author unthinkingly described a new line of products as having teething troubles, and in another report a colleague described the director of a bath and sink manufacturer as having been in baths for over twenty years. Watch for such howlers in your review.   5.3

c) Sentence components   Ref

It is not enough to know how to string together the main parts of the sentence. Each clause and   4.4b
phrase must itself be properly assembled, so you have to understand:

- the parts of speech (i.e. the types of word: noun, verb, adjective, adverb etc)
- their various forms (cases, tenses, participles etc)
- the relationships amongst them (which words to use with which other words)
- the rules covering how they are structured into phrases, clauses and sentences.

If you are not conversant with these elements, some extra study will remedy the situation. It   App
should be easier as an adult than it was as a school pupil, as you will recognise most of what you   4I
study, whereas for a pupil it is largely new ground. If you obtain a sound basic working knowledge of the four aspects listed above, you will be reasonably well equipped. Concentrate on the correct use of verbs and tenses.

d) Punctuation   Ref

After sentence structure, punctuation is the most misused aspect of grammar.

Punctuation marks complement the words themselves in dividing sentences into their component parts to give greater clarity of meaning. If you use the wrong punctuation, you can create a sentence with the wrong meaning. The full stop (period), colon, question mark, exclamation mark, quotation mark, slash and hyphen are in general reasonably well understood, but the following are often misapplied:

Semi-colon (;) This is used to connect two clauses without a conjunction; it can also connect phrases in a list. Two clauses may not be joined by a comma unless a conjunction (and, but, or, while, when etc) is used immediately after the comma.

Dash (-) This is technically not an English punctuation mark, but is used so often that it is now accepted as such. Used singly before a list, it acts as a colon, and used in pairs it acts as brackets. It can also introduce an addition at the end of a sentence - like this. Some software does not have separate symbols for a dash and a hyphen, so insert a space before and after a dash - like this - to distinguish it from the hyphen, which is non-spaced.   cont'd

The Report Report
Notes and Observations

d) Punctuation (continued)   Ref

Apostrophe (') This indicates a shortening of a word, especially with forms of the verbs 'to be' or 'to have' (e.g. *I'm, you've, he'll, we'd*). It is also used to indicate possession (e.g. *Gregory's Girl*), but not with pronouns (e.g. *yours, hers, its*). The word *it's* with an apostrophe is short for *it is*, or *it has*, but not for the possessive, *of it.*

Note that apostrophes should not be used to denote the plural, not even with abbreviations. Write 'PCs' and 'the 1960s' without apostrophes when you refer to them in the plural. Brand names such as Levi's and Jack Daniel's indicate possession, not plurality, so it is correct to write a 'pair of Levi's' [jeans], although it appears odd.

Comma (,) The humble comma is a simple separator, but is misused to a bewildering extent, even by allegedly erudite newspapers. Its proper uses are:

- to separate phrases, in a sentence
- to separate clauses, when used with a conjunction (the purpose is to emphasise the separation, as a conjunction alone will usually suffice)
- to separate words in a list (phrases in a list are usually separated by semi-colons)
- in pairs, to separate a phrase 'in parenthesis', rather like a mild form of brackets.

Note that in the bullet-point list format used above, this report does not use punctuation at the end of each point (except the final one). This is because the bullets effectively punctuate the list. Bullets, like dashes, are not officially regarded as punctuation, but are so useful and so clear in layout that they are used frequently.

Commas are not used in the following situations:

- between a verb and its subject, except when a pair are used, almost as brackets
   The team manager up in the stand, ordered a substitution. single - incorrect
   The team manager, up in the stand, ordered a substitution. pair - acceptable

- between the last two items in a list, where a conjunction is used
   Crosby, Stills, Nash & Young (the '&' may only be used in names and headings)
   beg, borrow or steal

Note that it has become fashionable for business enterprises to omit punctuation from their names, so check whether your report should be addressed to AU Geldof McLeod & Co or to A.U. Geldof, McLeod & Co. And is it Co or Co. or Company?

Real life: *A small country railway depot was to be demolished, except for the station building, the signal box and the bridge over the still-active tracks. A careless person in the demolition company issued a written instruction to demolish 'everything except the station bridge and signal box'. Because there was no comma between 'station' and 'bridge' to indicate that they were separate structures, the demolition team thought that only the 'station bridge' and signal box were to be left standing, and duly demolished everything else. The company was made to rebuild the old station house, stone by stone, to its exact original construction. Punctuation matters.*

A full explanation of grammar needs a whole textbook in itself. If you are reporting on a regular basis at a level which demands a high quality of narrative, you must have a strong grasp of at least the fundamentals of grammar, to the extent where you instinctively know what is correct and what is not. If you do not have this, then undertake a course of classes; it is essential if your reports are to be clear and credible.

If you at least get the above basics right, you are less likely to say or write such gems as 'a friend of my wife, who is insufferable...' and 'I have wanted to see the dentist for two months'.

The Report Report
Notes and Observations

An organisation can have an overall culture, particularly if the organisation is a small one. But the larger an organisation becomes, the more you are likely to find several cultures existing. These can consist of different cultures in different parts of the organisation, and even a combination of cultures existing in the same part. Below are listed some of the common cultures you are likely to encounter. The list concentrates on adverse cultures rather than favourable ones, since adverse cultures are the ones likely to cause you difficulty when you are gathering information and later trying to express your findings and opinions accurately and unequivocally but diplomatically in your report.

a) General cultures - existing throughout an organisation

Ignorance - some organisations are blissfully ignorant of the outside world, and even ignorant of the fact that they are ignorant. They have probably survived through a combination of lucky circumstances and because they are not perceived as a threat to any competing organisations.

Complacency - this is a much worse culture than ignorance, because people in the organisation have actually considered their circumstances, and yet still do not believe that action is necessary.

Know-it-all - this is an aggravated form of complacency.

Not invented here - this appears to be a know-it-all culture, but it is not. It arises because an organisation (often with some justification) has a fierce pride and belief in the way it operates, and is therefore sceptical of any alternative methods or products. The culture is acceptable if due thought is given to any external methods or products, but if they are written off automatically as inferior, the culture is damaging, as it eventually leads to complacency.

Family - a difficult environment in which to work. In family organisations, structures and decisions can arise from a host of reasons which bear no direct relation to the needs of the organisation. Moreover, there is a reluctance within the organisation to explain these hidden agendas to outsiders. Reporting on any aspect of a family organisation may therefore be a difficult task even if the subject is straightforward.

Formality - provided that it is not excessive, this is not a problem. But in an over-formal culture, people are likely to be inhibited in their working relationships and may not develop the degree of cooperation and trust needed for a fully-effective team.

Informality - generally less of a danger than formality, since morale and team spirit are likely to be higher than in a formal organisation, and people are likely to enjoy their work more (you can expect frequent laughter in the workplace). But if the informality is maintained at the expense of discipline, the organisation can perform sloppily.

Detail - some organisations, especially younger ones and technically-oriented ones, are obsessed with detail. As a result, meetings can take forever and leaders can lose sight of their main objectives and fail to address major issues adequately. The opposite culture, inattention to detail, is less common, since leaders who are focused on the 'big picture' tend to be good delegators, and ensure that details are attended to at an appropriate level. However, 'big picture' leaders who change their priorities frequently are apt to forget that they have to adjust the organisational structure to cope with the corresponding changes in detail, and a backlog of unresolved details tends to build up, sometimes with serious consequences.

The Report Report
Notes and Observations

b) Horizontal cultures - affecting relations across an organization

Territoriality - a classic sign of insecurity, even at high levels. Insecure people are overly conscious of boundaries between territories, departments and other divisions of an organisation. They will claim ownership or credit for everything they regard as part of their territory, and be quick to attribute any responsibilities or misdemeanours to other territories. It goes without saying that this is a destructive culture, and it often indicates a failure of higher management in allowing it to develop.

Competitiveness - this sounds like the kind of culture one should encourage, but internal competitiveness is only acceptable if it does not restrict internal cooperation. When competitiveness gets out of hand, it can result in a perception of colleagues as enemies. Each division of an organisation should try to be the most effective division as a matter of pride, but not at the expense of helping the other divisions.

Compartmentalisation - this happens when departments become compartments, and is more commonly found in large organisations which become over-structured. Even a simple task then becomes a major operation if it involves two or more departments.

Dominance of one faction or discipline - an organisation can be dominated by one particular type of person. They may be from a discipline such as finance or marketing, or from a particular social, academic, organisational or other background. Sometimes this is only a perceived dominance rather than a real one, but either way it can create counter-productive attitudes and prejudices within the organisation.

Post-merger hangover - after the merger of two or more organisations, careless management can allow a two-tier situation to form, in which the remnants of one of the original organisations regard the others as inferior. The resentment can cause the cultures of the original organisations to continue separately for years after the merger.

Whipping-boy - in many groups of people engaged in a serious purpose, a 'whipping-boy' emerges, who is the butt of all derogatory comments. The whipping-boy is often an entire department whose performance is continually derided by the others. Once this culture is established, the whipping-boy tends to be castigated even when he performs well. It takes a great deal of sustained management effort to reverse such an attitude in the rest of the organisation.

Discrimination - whether this is by race, religion, sex or any other criterion, it is not only invidious, but stupid. For example, discriminating against either sex when recruiting or promoting may deprive one of a large percentage of the talent available for the particular task. We all have our likes and dislikes, but when dislikes become institutionalised they can seriously erode the performance of an organisation. People indulge in senseless vendettas and deliberate impeding of the activities of those against whom they are discriminating. The report writer interviewing for information is likely to hear endless tales of woe and bitterness and when he eventually does elicit some information, he will have little confidence in its impartiality.

Meeting aversion or obsession - 'We see each other every day, so we don't need meetings' may be true of a very small organisation, but communication deteriorates as the organisation grows and structured meetings become essential. At the other end of the spectrum, some organisations spend so much time in meetings that their output of profitable action is well below requirements. The reporter can gauge the effectiveness of the meetings by examining the minutes, reports and memos arising from the meetings and asking for evidence (preferably measurement) of the resulting actions.

c) **Vertical cultures - affecting relations up and down an organisation**

Dominant chief executive (or commander, or whatever) - this culture starts when a particularly strong character is surrounded by a diffident team, and it develops in the mind of the dominator to a state of contempt for his subordinates. It usually ends in the belief of the dominator of his invincibility. In any organisation where you have an unchecked leader, you have a problem which if allowed to continue may spell the end of the organisation. Strong leadership requires a strong leader with a strong team who are not afraid to challenge the leader, while still respecting his authority. A leader who cannot effectively handle challenges from his subordinates is fundamentally weak, even though he may appear strong.

Dominant or remote (in attitude) headquarters - not as bad as the above, but nevertheless a problem. It is usually caused by not having sufficient front-line experience amongst headquarters personnel to enable them to put strategic direction into a practical context and link effectively in both directions with the front-line units.

Outpost - often in reaction to an under-performing head office, a distant unit will cut itself off as far as possible from the rest of the organisation. This may be good or bad.

Trapdoor - another characteristic of insecurity. Promoted people fail to develop their subordinates in case they become a threat. The resulting frustration is felt most keenly by the high-calibre subordinates, who are usually the first to leave, often with rancour.

These and other cultures may affect the way you perform your reporting work. You should not become personally involved in cultural aspects, but you need to be aware of how they affect the accuracy of the information given to you, and the performance of the organisation or parts of it on which you are reporting. Moreover, you need to write your report in a style which displays your impartiality and which covers the relevant points in a way acceptable to the addressees.

Where there are inbuilt prejudices, you must be doubly sure that you have good evidence to support your findings and conclusions, as they will be challenged strongly when they go against the prejudices.

Section 4.1b discusses how to deal with cultural issues when reporting.

The Report Report
Notes and Observations

Words are ever more frequently misused as education concentrates increasingly on technical matters. There is little point in being technically proficient, however, unless you can communicate your thoughts clearly, so here are some typical errors. Today's errors may become tomorrow's idiom, but for the time being they are errors.

Don't say	When you mean	Because
gender	sex	gender is a grammatical term which applies to words - for example, a German of the female sex starts life in the neuter gender (das Kind, das Fräulein) then, when she marries or reaches 'a certain age', takes the female gender (die Frau). Gender is less prominent in English - however, a ship is of the female gender ('she') but is neuter in sex.
less	fewer	if you can count them, use fewer (less sugar, fewer grains of sugar) but do not use fewer for measurements - Ben Nevis is less (not fewer) than 1,500 metres high
due to	owing to	due to means 'caused by' and relates to a noun - the delay (noun) was due to (caused by) fog; owing to (the correct phrase in nine cases out of ten) means 'because of' and relates to a verb - we were delayed (verb) owing to (because of) fog
verbal	oral or spoken	verbal means 'in words' and can mean written or spoken words
exotic	unusual	exotic means 'from another country' - something exotic can be very ordinary
practical	practicable	people are practical (by nature) if their ideas are practicable (capable of being put into practice)
decimate	nearly eliminate	to decimate means to cut the head off every tenth person - a Roman legion custom to improved performance in a modern sense it means to reduce by 10%
appraise	apprise	to appraise someone means to review his performance with him to apprise someone means to inform him (most commonly in the context of a situation update)
upstanding	standing up	upstanding people are people of high moral character, even when they are sitting or lying down
dependant	dependent	a dependant is someone who is dependent on someone else (but independent always has an 'e' for some reason)
cohort	assistant	a cohort is a group, usually of soldiers - it does not mean an individual person
fine toothcomb	fine-toothed comb	a common howler - most people brush their teeth, but does anybody comb them?
disinterested	uninterested	uninterested means having no interest, but disinterested means impartial - a disinterested person can be very interested

Having spent most of the 20th century shortening English terms to make them sound slicker, US Americans are now unnecessarily lengthening them to make them sound more technical. The British have caught the habit. Unfortunately, it can result in words which don't mean what they're supposed to.

Don't say	When you mean	Because
methodology	method	method already is an 'ology'
epicentre	centre	the epicentre of an object is the point on the surface closest to the centre - it can be a long way from the centre
transportation	transport	transport already is a noun - transportation is therefore like locationation, which is of course nonsense
infrastructure	structure	an infrastructure is a structure beyond or below the structure - e.g. the rail system or the sewage system
subcontractor	contractor	a subcontractor is a contractor to your contractor
Indian subcontinent	India	the subcontinent includes other nations such as Pakistan, Bangladesh and the Himalayan states
fiefdom	fief	a fief is a 'dom'
meaningfulness	meaning	meaningful is the adjective from meaning, so don't add anything further to make it a noun again

THE REPORT REPORT
4. STYLE
4B COMMONLY MISUSED WORDS

App 4B

The Report Report
Notes and Observations

4C WORDS DENOTING SIZE OR IMPORTANCE

Real life: A major consultancy firm prepared a tender for a wide range of financial and related services. Each section of the tender was prepared by the relevant department of the firm, and the whole draft was submitted for review. A reviewer found that whenever a word meaning 'large' or 'important' was needed, the word 'significant', very much the yuppie word of the time, had been entered. Considering that this major proposal was a showcase of the firm's reporting ability, the potential client was hardly likely to be impressed with a document containing the word 'significant' over 100 times.

In fact, 'significant' does not necessarily mean large. For example, an error in a computer printout can be very small, but highly significant in that it indicates a fault in a critical control procedure, or the possibility of deliberate corruption. If you feel an irresistible urge to write 'significant', think about the alternatives below. The tables are by no means exhaustive, but they cover most of the expressions likely to be suitable, and a few that should be avoided.

Expressions which mean 'BIG'

big, large	sizeable	bulky	wide-ranging	outsize(d)
major	substantial	spacious	far-reaching	oversize(d)
wide	considerable	capacious	all-embracing	over-large
long, lengthy	appreciable	voluminous	all-encompassing	excessive
high, tall, deep	large-scale	extensive	comprehensive	overweight

Expressions meaning 'IMPORTANT' (not necessarily big)

significant	paramount	necessary	radical
critical	crucial	essential	fundamental
heavy	key	vital	central
major	decisive	mission-critical	

Expressions likely to be overstatement and/or colloquial, and therefore to be generally avoided

enormous	colossal	huge	vast	giant, gigantic
titanic	gargantuan	massive	immense	stupendous
monstrous	megalithic	king-sized	jumbo-sized	monumental

Adverbs accentuating adjectives, usually unnecessarily

very	highly	greatly	totally	much [more/less]
significantly	seriously	deeply	utterly	many [more/fewer]

It is usually sufficient to use an adjective without an adverb such as those above to enhance it. For example, saying 'this machinery is dangerous' is likely to have more impact than saying 'this machinery is highly dangerous'.

In particular, avoid using the word 'totally' to indicate extent unless you really do mean '100%'. For example, the statement that a car is 'totally underpowered' means that it does not have an engine. Calling someone 'totally dishonest' means that every statement he makes is a lie, which is unlikely.

Finally, avoid the word 'never'. It is an absolute word, meaning 'not once - ever' and should not be applied to a finite period, such as 'never in five years'. You are almost always better to use the word 'not', which does not pretend an absolute knowledge of all time.

The Report Report
Notes and Observations

4D PADDING - UNNECESSARY WORDS

We all use padding in conversation. Why? Perhaps we think it makes what we are saying sound more polite or more sophisticated, or less blunt. Perhaps we are just subconsciously copying others, sheep that we are. Padding has infiltrated written English to an alarming degree and no matter how hard you try not to use it you will find when you review your work carefully that you have to cut out a surprising number of words. Here are two examples, the first one from real life.

Extract from a CV (résumé)

Jun 99 - present: Currently employed by Teknik Factors Ltd of Smallburgh as Personal Assistant to the Chief Executive of the company, which sells engineering supplies. My rôle involves conventional administrative and secretarial duties in the head office, and liaison with the sales force to analyse demand for products and predict future sales trends.

The words underlined are either repetitive or already understood in the context of the CV:

- *'present' and 'currently' mean the same*
- *'employed' is obvious from the context*
- *'of the company' is obvious in the context*
- *'my rôle involves' is what a CV is all about anyway*
- *'conventional' is understood for the duties described*
- *'in the head office' is where a chief executive normally works*
- *'the' is unnecessary when writing in note form (as opposed to prose)*
- *'predict' is about the future, so 'future sales trends' is superfluous*

Delete these words and you have a shorter, more direct paragraph. Using this process, the writer was able to reduce her CV from three to two pages, greatly increasing the impact of the document without removing any information. She had a new job within five weeks.

Jun 99 - present: Teknik Factors Ltd, engineering parts supplier, Smallburgh - Personal Assistant to Chief Executive. Administrative and secretarial duties, and liaison with sales force to analyse and predict demand for products.

General example

Once you have had the opportunity to meet with your team and discuss with them the contents of our report, we should meet at a mutually convenient date in order to agree the courses of action to be taken to resolve the issues which we have raised. [47 words]

The following words can be removed without loss of meaning:
- *'have had the opportunity to' - waffle*
- *'meet with your team and discuss' - if they're discussing, they're meeting (even if it's by telephone) and the word 'with' is always superfluous in that context ('meet up with' is even worse)*
- *'the contents of' - well, what else would they discuss?'*
- *at a mutually convenient date' - if we have to meet, we have to meet*
- *'in order' - unnecessary*
- *'courses of action' - classic padding; 'actions' will do*
- *'to be taken' - unnecessary, but could be shortened to 'needed' if you really want it*
- *'which' - not strictly necessary; it can be understood without being written, but*
- *the issues 'which we have raised' - this whole phrase does not add anything, since the issues obviously stem from our report.*

Once you have discussed our report with your team we should meet to agree the actions needed. [17 words - no loss of meaning despite reduction of the sentence by nearly two thirds]

The Report Report
Notes and Observations

Tautology (also called redundancy) is a combination of two words or phrases which mean the same. Not only is it nonsensical, it is pompous and a waste of words. Here are some common examples.

Don't say	Say	Because
deliberate attempt	attempt	an attempt is a deliberate action (except where deliberate means methodical)
conscious decision	decision	a decision is a conscious process
completely unanimous	unanimous	unanimous means in complete agreement
completely unique	unique	if something is unique, there is only one of it - it can't be more or less unique, but it can be unique in more or fewer respects
too much is bad for you	a lot is bad for you	if it is bad for you, it must be too much
fastest speed	highest speed	speed is a measure of fastness
slowest speed	lowest speed	speed is a measure of slowness
deepest depth	greatest depth	same principle - for words denoting measurement, such as height, depth, width, weight, rate etc,use greater/greatest and lesser/least for comparison
the reason is because	it is because, or the reason is	reason and cause mean the same
reverse back	go back, or reverse	to reverse is to go back
raise it up, lower it down	raise it, lower it	raise it means take it up, lower it means bring it down
enter into	enter	enter means go into
come back again	come back, or come again	back and again mean the same - to come back again is to come a third time
repeat that again	repeat that, or do that again	repeat and again have the same meaning - to repeat an action again is to do it for the third time
potential threat	threat	a threat is a potential danger
future potential	potential	potential refers to the future
future plans	plans	plans in this context are about the future anyway (but if the plans have not yet been made, it may make sense to describe them as future plans)
past experience	experience	if it's experience, it's in the past
past history	history	ditto
recommend that you should do	recommend that you do	should is inherent in a recommendation or a suggestion
declare UDI	declare UI	the D in UDI stands for declaration
it would appear [that]	it appears [that]	appear already expresses uncertainty
it would seem to appear	it appears	are you an accountant by any chance? *
outstanding debt	debt	if it's debt, it's outstanding - and vice versa *
at this moment in time	now, just now	this moment is a time, and the phrase is pompous

* Accountants - tautologists extraordinary

The Report Report prize for applied tautology goes to the accountant who prepared a list of liabilities, the last of which he described as 'Estimated provision for contingencies (say) £50,000'.

'Contingencies £50,000' would have sufficed.

The Report Report

'The Report Report' is not tautology, because it is a report (specific) on reports (in general).

The Report Report
Notes and Observations

The following words are frequently used in the plural form as if they were singular. You should say "the media are" not "the media is", because the media consist of several mediums (press, radio, television). The same goes for the other words. It is illogical to talk of "a criteria" or "a phenomena"; it is equivalent to talking of "a cattle" or "a houses".

Singular - one only (with "is" or "was")	Plural - more than one (with "are" or "were")
criterion	criteria
phenomenon	phenomena
medium	media
datum	data
none (which means "not one")	there is no plural for this - how can there be?
there is no singular for this	premises (meaning land and buildings)
bacterium	bacteria
cherub	cherubim
seraph	seraphim
Bedou or Bedu	Bedouin
(caution - this can be derogatory in the singular)	

The following are examples of **collective nouns** - words which are singular, but which refer to a collection of items and are therefore have a plural inference. There are hundreds of such nouns, and you may treat them grammatically as singular or plural. Singular is technically more correct, but plural sometimes sounds better, especially in spoken English. You can say "the committee meets" (singular) or "the committee meet" (plural). Whichever form you choose, use it throughout your report.

country	industry	group	board	population	box
region	market	division	committee	portfolio	rack
town	trade	company	team	batch	shipment
community	sector	branch	department	sample	lot

The following words in the left-hand column should only be used in relation to a choice of two items. If there are three or more items, use the words in the right-hand column

Two items only	More than two items
former	first
latter	last
between	among, amongst
either	one of
neither	not, none of
both	all
comparatives	superlatives
(better, worse, greener)	(best, worst, greenest)

The Report Report
Notes and Observations

There are many different ways of saying the same thing. How you say it is important in three ways.

- *It affects how clearly or otherwise you get your message across.*
- *It can influence the relationship between you and the addressee.*
- *It says a lot about you - your maturity, your judgment, your intellect, your capability.*

These aspects gain especial importance when what you are saying is contentious. The examples below, which compare replies to an unwelcome proposal, illustrate the range of expression open to you.

1. Your proposal is utterly disgraceful, totally unacceptable and an insult to common decency. I shall oppose it in the strongest terms and do my utmost to ensure that others do the same.

Bombastic. You can almost see this person, red-faced and puffing out his chest, albeit with the most honourable of intentions. Such pompous wording is often the output of people who have gained a position of responsibility by honest efforts, but who lack the finesse, particularly of language, to make the most of their position. The proposer will smile when he receives this response and know that he is in no danger. Ammunition which has been fired is no longer ammunition.

2. I don't like what you're suggesting. It stinks.

This is conversational language, the effect of which is uncertain. It is more threatening to the proposer than example 1, and has the advantage of not telling the proposer what the objector intends to do. It may worry the proposer a little, but unless he has a specific reason to fear the writer he will assume that it is merely a grumpy emotional response, and go ahead with the proposal.

3. I regret to advise you that I shall not be supporting your proposal, as I consider it to be an extreme measure in the circumstances. I believe that most others will take the same stance.

The measured, unemotional tone suggests a stronger opponent who has thought out his position more carefully. The reply does not confront the proposer outright and yet contains a degree of menace, in that the writer appears to know more about the general viewpoint than the proposer does. Moreover, the fact that the writer uses understated language, unlike writer no 1, indicates that he is confident of his views and dismissive of the proposer. The proposer will be on his guard with this person.

4. I fully understand what you are seeking to achieve through your proposal. However, some aspects of it are expressed in a way which could alienate the public and thus greatly impair your chances of success. I have time available this week and would welcome the chance to discuss these aspects with you to try and present them in a way which will readily find general acceptance.

This writer appears to be sympathising with the proposer... but in fact he is not. He realises that proposer is in a strong position, and that the only way to deflect him is to work alongside him rather than against him. In reviewing the proposal with the proposer, he will have the chance to instil concerns in the mind of the proposer with regard to the people who will be voting on it. The writer may even be skilful enough to manoeuvre the proposer into diluting the proposal sufficiently to satisfy everyone. But to get alongside the proposer in the first place, the writer has to create the impression of being an ally.

The occasion needing the most careful choice of style is that of attributing blame. Your choice of words ranges from a full condemnation to a virtual evasion by mentioning the problem but not the guilty party:

Extreme	the Council had full knowledge of their responsibility for the property and of the danger to it, but despite that, they failed to act to prevent the damage; they are guilty of gross negligence
Severe	the Council had full knowledge of the danger and yet failed to act to prevent the damage
Fairly severe	although aware of the danger, the Council did not prevent the damage
Straightforward	the Council did not prevent the damage
Mild	no action was taken to prevent the damage *(the use of the passive avoids naming anyone)*
Evasive	the property was not subject to any protection and thus was damaged *(the passive again)*

The Report Report
Notes and Observations

It is not possible to define an appropriate style for each set of circumstances. However, the styles discussed in the examples below should be avoided in all reports, unless you are deliberately trying to antagonise the addressees, which is likely to harm you more than them.

Condescension - being patronising is more likely to occur in speech, usually preceded by 'irritators'.

- *For my sins...* someone is about to boast about being chairman of something irrelevant.
- *I hear what you say, but...* someone is not in the least interested in what you are saying.
- *I always take the view that...* someone thinks his reasoning is infallible, whatever the facts are.

Note that all of the above involve the first person singular. If you do not use *I, me* or *my* in writing your report, you are unlikely to express yourself condescendingly, unless it is deliberate.

Pomposity - Dickensian language is still used by many in letter-writing in the mistaken belief that it is correct practice. It can also spill over into reporting language. Good English is straightforward English, so keep it simple at all times. Here are some examples:

Pompous	Straightforward
I am in receipt of your letter of 12th inst	Thank you for your letter of 12 [name of month]
Please find enclosed	I enclose
We beg to advise you that X has happened	X has happened
It would appear / it would seem to appear	It appears
I remain, yours faithfully	Yours faithfully
At your earliest convenience	As soon as possible / as soon as you can
Assuring you of our best attention at all times	Please let us know if we can be of further help

Note that some pompous wording tends also to be grovelling, which has no place in any report. You are writing from a position of authority, even though you are providing a service. Most pompous wording also has a strong element of padding, and you can avoid it by stating matters as simply as possible.

Buzzwords - these are pieces of jargon and other current phrases on their way to becoming clichés, and are used at all levels in organisations. As with jargon, they are the refuge of insecure people, who feel they must use the latest expressions to demonstrate their awareness. But it backfires on them, because anybody who tries to be cool is by definition not cool at all. However, older sayings which have ceased to be trendy can be useful, provided that they are relevant and used sparingly. For instance, when an organisation changes its structure to suit its computer systems instead of the other way around, the phrase 'the tail is wagging the dog' may be appropriate. The ridiculous picture it evokes puts the situation in perspective without being unduly critical.

Destructive criticism - criticism is often a prominent function of a report, and it must therefore be made fairly and maturely. It must not be destructive. There are rules.

- Avoid emotional language and any hint of personal feeling.
- Concentrate strictly on the action being criticised and the reason for its inadequacy.
- Where possible, state what should be done instead of the action being criticized.
- If you have no alternative to offer, do not criticise directly - instead, advise that *you need an alternative method of...* or similar wording. If you do not know the answer, you have no right to be critical, but you are entitled to highlight the need for action

At all times, show respect for human dignity; apart from the fact that there is no need for disrespect, you may have to work with the person you have criticised, to remedy the problem.

Sarcasm or flippancy - when we are young, we think we know everything, and then we mature and realise how much we don't know. Then when we have been around a long time, we begin to think again that we know everything. In these younger and older stages we are most likely to use sarcasm, which is a particularly British form of humour, and funny only if it is intelligent and spoken. In writing, it is normally destructive and should be avoided. Flippancy is a light form of sarcasm which tends to come across as a 'cheap shot' and should also be avoided. If you must use this approach, restrict it to mild irony (4.1f).

The Report Report
Notes and Observations

The Chambers Dictionary (Chambers Harrap)
Recognised throughout the world by users at every level as the finest single-volume dictionary of the English language. Beautifully presented and printed, with full and precise meanings for words ranging from the ancient to the very modern, including abbreviations and common foreign expressions.

Roget's Thesaurus (various editions - Penguin recommended)
A remarkable work, giving synonyms and word equivalents rather than meanings. Essential when you're looking for a word which means "something like . . .", but be sure to check the exact meaning of your chosen word in the dictionary as well. Ask for the edition with the alphabetical word list.

Style Guide (Economist Books)
If The Report Report gives you a cake, the Style Guide will put the icing on it. How to state things, how not to state them, grammar, punctuation, common errors, international names and facts and a host of other useful information for the serious report writer.

The Complete Plain Words (Penguin)
Somewhere between The Report Report and The Style Guide in territory, Plain Words was written by Sir Ernest Gowers and is a model of clarity. Useful for any report-writer.

The Penguin Dictionary of Language (Penguin)
By David Crystal - a powerful little encyclopædia for the serious international reporter. It covers the mechanics of the English language and gives much information on the world's other languages.

Mother Tongue (Penguin)
Bill Bryson's erudite and entertaining examination of the development of the English language from its Latin, German, French and other sources, and of the parallel developments of UK and US English.

Difficult Words (Penguin)
Bill Bryson again - for those who have trouble in distinguishing "celebrant" from "celebrator", this book explains the differences in meanings between commonly confused words.

http://owl.english.purdue.edu/handouts/print/index.html
It is difficult to find a suitable English grammar textbook for adults, but this website gives you specific answers and simple, crisp examples to most grammar questions and many other queries you may have about writing. It is presented by OWL, the Online Writing Lab, and is easy to navigate. Worth a visit.

The Oxford Dictionary of Quotations (Oxford University Press)
The Report Report recommends that you avoid using quotations. Nevertheless, to become an effective writer, you must be a retentive reader, and this allows you to dip into the works of accomplished writers and speakers and absorb their skills and rhythms a little at a time. If you use a quotation which is still subject to copyright, you should attribute it to the original writer or speaker.

Bad Lies in Business (McGraw-Hill)
An extraordinary and humorous book by fraud and security prevention experts Mike Comer, David Price and Patrick Ardis. It covers interview and investigation techniques, with emphasis on detecting and eliminating deceit using subtle but common-sense methods. Fascinating.

Numbers Guide (Economist Books)
Although it is financially oriented, it contains copious information on the interpretation, use and presentation of statistics of all kinds. For those dealing in serious numbers.

Marketing Plans (Butterworth Heinemann)
Written by Malcolm McDonald, this is the bible of marketing strategy, essential reading for all company directors. But that is not why it is included here; it is a shining example of how to present information by intelligent use of graphics and tables, and is worth buying for that alone if you write complex reports.

THE REPORT REPORT

The Report Report
Notes and Observations

At last we are on to the most enjoyable part. You have worked out what you need to say, how to say it and what layout to use, and you now have to manage the process of bringing your information together into a report. The process is like any other project and production process; the more systematically you do it, the fewer hitches you will have and the more you will enjoy the process.

SUMMARY

	Ref
The design process crystallises the thought you have given to the content and layout of your report.	5.1a
▪ List the section and subsection headings you need.	5.1b
▪ From the point of view of the addressees, read through the headings, checking that they flow in a natural and logical sequence.	5.1b
▪ Apply numbering to the section and subsection headings.	5.1c
▪ On a large notepad, write each section heading at the top of a fresh page.	5.1d
▪ On each page, write the subsection headings, widely spaced, down the left side.	5.1d
▪ Under each subsection heading, write the topic headings.	5.1d
▪ If your report requires an information-gathering exercise, write the topic headings before you start collecting information, so that you have a numbered filing system ready to receive the information.	5.1e
▪ Design your page format according to your chosen layout.	5.1f
▪ When you have written the first one or two subsections, check that your layout meets your needs - minor amendments may be needed.	5.1f

a) Objectives

	Ref

The objectives of the design stage are to ensure that:

▪ you include all the content which you have determined that you need	2.1-4
▪ you lay it out in the form and sequence you have chosen	3.1-5
▪ you can give your writing your full attention without having to return continually to amend your framework (a frustrating process)	4.1-4

b) Overall content

	Ref

List the main sections of your report needed to satisfy the addressee's remit. Remember the rule of fives. — 3.2b

Then break each main section heading down into subsection headings, again remembering the rule of fives. — 3.2b

Arrange your proposed headings and sub-headings into the order in which they appear to flow naturally. Check that the sequence is correct from the point of view of the addressees, ie that the information is revealed to them in the order in which they need it, taking into account what they know already. They should not have to read anything which is not explained until later in the report, except for introductory remarks made at the beginning of a subsection. — 3.1b

You may find later as you are writing the report that you have to adjust the order again in one or two places. Do not worry about that; it shows that you are thinking carefully about what you are writing.

The Report Report
Notes and Observations

c) Numbering

Ref

Once you are satisfied with the content, its sections and its sequence, give the report and each section a provisional contents list. Even though you may amend this later, you need a framework within which to work, and the numbering helps considerably.

3.2

Remember that detail which is essential or useful but which by its nature interrupts the flow of the report should probably be assigned to an appendix.

3.2k

d) Detailed content

Ref

Take your laptop or a pad of notepaper and allocate a sheet to each section. At wide intervals down the left hand side write your headings for the subsections in each section. Allocate another sheet for the headings of the appendices.

1.4a
3.2k

Now write the names of the detailed topics you wish to include in each subsection. It helps if you approach this section by section, but inevitably you will think of items to be included in other sections. Write them down immediately under the relevant headings.

1.4a

Keep your notepad (in whatever form) of topic headings with you at all times during the reporting process. You will find that you continue to think of additional items to be included, or amendments to be made, and you need to be able to note these immediately or you will forget them.

As you write the report you will find that some of the topics you have noted are better included in different subsections from the ones in which you listed them. Do not rub out the notes, but cross out the original entries and write them under the preferred subsection headings. Do not worry if a topic crops up in more than one part of the report, but ensure that the treatment of it is not over-repetitive.

e) Information control

Ref

If your remit involves an information-gathering project, such as an investigation of any kind, culminating in a report on your findings, you should design the report contents page before you even start the project.

3.2

Why? Because in designing the layout of your end product:

- you will naturally organise your information-gathering process in the same logical way, thereby saving a considerable amount of time
- you will have a filing index (i.e. your report index) already established in which your information can be stored as soon as it is gathered
- the report index will act as a check-list, so that you can monitor progress and will be unlikely to miss any areas in your investigation
- designing the report structure will highlight any major gaps or queries regarding the remit, and these can be clarified at an early stage, impressing the addressees with your foresight and avoiding blind alleys and missed areas

2.1

- you should be able to begin detailed reporting in some subsections while information-gathering is still proceeding in others, thereby reducing the overall time taken by the project

However tempting it may be to begin gathering information immediately, you will do it more quickly and effectively if you design the contents page first.

The Report Report
Notes and Observations

f) Blank format (template)

Ref

Once you have completed your basic design, draw up a blank page format or template if you are using a word processor. As an example, the format used in this report is shown at the back of this section. Ensure that the blank contains printing and other default settings (font, spelling etc) so that you do not have to repeat these for each page or subsection.

App
5A

When you have finished writing the first one or two draft subsections, review them for appearance and make any necessary amendments to the blank page format. Then copy it, head it and number it for each of your proposed sections and subsections.

5.3e

Whenever you start writing any part of the report you will thus have a numbered format in place for it, and your report will take shape in the designed format from the beginning, with a minimum of subsequent amendment.

g) Report title

Ref

The title of your report may have been decided at the remit stage. If not, you usually have plenty of time to consider it. In general, start with a working title on the basis of "Report to Addressees on [Subject] by [Writer]". It may also be necessary to include a date in the title if the subject relates only to a certain date or period. If the date is not in the title, it should be noted prominently in the introduction.

2.1

1.1

The part of the title dealing with the subject should be specific, but brief. There are reports with titles like "Report to The Research Council on the incidence of Weissner's Phenomenon as evidenced by readings taken under controlled conditions from May 200X to July 200Y" but such reports tend to be esoteric, and not for general purposes. If you do need a long title, split it into a short main heading ("Incidence of Weissner's Phenomenon") in large print, and show the detail in smaller print below. Users then have the option of using only the main heading when referring to it.

1.1/2

Once you are well into the reporting process, you may wish to amend your working title or replace it altogether with something more distinctive. Do not make the title any longer than it need be. "Proposal for ring road for Shugborough" will suffice if it is the only proposal and everyone concerned is aware of the situation. Reports for internal use in an organisation likewise only need short titles in many cases, such as "Review of storage life of paints". But a title like "Budget 200Y" can be confusing if your financial year-end is 31 January 200Y, and most of the figures therefore apply to the year 200X. Ensure that the title is unequivocal as well as brief.

You may prefer a more marketable title if you wish your report to catch the imagination of a wide readership. Titles like "The way forward" and "A new approach" have been over-used by now, but there is still infinite scope for you to apply your imagination.

Finally, bear in mind that the title does not have to include the word "Report". Titles such as "Communities - Power to the People?" or "Transport - Roadblock Ahead" can be effective attention-grabbers and are easily remembered. Whatever you do, ensure that the title is relevant, and not likely to antagonise the people you wish to influence.

The design process completes your preparation, and now is the time to begin writing. Go for it.

The Report Report
Notes and Observations

Your design process is the distillation of your entire planning process, and with the framework in place you are ready to begin writing. It may seem to have taken a long time to get to this stage, but the result will be worth it.

SUMMARY

Ref

Having organised yourself and structured your thoughts to a high degree in the initial considerations and the design process, you can allow yourself comparative freedom in the writing process to ensure a smooth flow of thoughts on to paper.

- Just before starting writing, remind yourself of the style you intend to use. | 5.2b
- Draft the introductory section first, to point your thoughts in the right direction. | 5.2c
- When writing the main body of the report, choose the easiest sections first to build up your momentum and confidence. | 5.2d
- Write appendices whenever you wish, as they are not essential to the flow. | 5.2e
- Choose whatever working routine suits you, but be disciplined and target yourself with a certain output per day. | 5.2f
- When you have a highly productive patch, extend it for as long as you can. | 5.2g
- Similarly, when your writing is not going well, transfer to another part of the report, and if that does not help, take a break and do something different. | 5.2h
- Ensure that all parallel processes, especially information gathering, are proceeding on schedule, so that you are not held up by any bottlenecks. | 5.2j
- Ensure that whatever technology you use can be operated by the publishers and printers of your report. | 5.2k
- If you are using software, back up your data regularly off-site. | 5.2k

a) Objective

Ref

The objective of your writing process is to ensure that you put on paper what you intended to report in the first place, in the manner in which you intended. Your writing habits therefore need to be disciplined and yet comfortable.

All

b) Style

Ref

Before you hit the keyboard, remind yourself one more time of the style in which you intend to write the report. Once your narrative has begun to flow, you will find it difficult to transfer to another style. Remember also which tenses etc you have decided to use.

4.2

4.2g

c) Introduction

Ref

Try and write the objectives, scope and definition subsections of the introduction before you write anything else. They are often the most unexciting sections to write, but writing them will help fix your commitments to your addressees firmly in your mind and point you in the right direction.

1.1/2
/4

1.3

From information you have gathered, you may be able to draft some of your conclusions and recommendations at the start of the writing process, and that may serve as a reminder that you have to provide adequate evidence for these in the body of the report. However, it is usually easier to complete these subsections at the end of the reporting process, when your thoughts have been fully documented and ordered.

cont'd

The Report Report
Notes and Observations

c) Introduction (continued)   Ref

When you have drafted the introduction as far as you can, print it out and give it an initial   5.3c
review. Check:

- is the content broadly what you intended?
- is the style appropriate for the context?
- is the page layout satisfactory? (make any amendments to the blank template now, to save repetition)

Once you are satisfied that you are heading in the right direction, start writing the body of the report.

d) Main content   Ref

When you start on the body of the report, write the easiest subsections first. These are usually the sections on which your ideas are already best formed. Occasionally, though, you can have a glut of ideas on a subject and find it difficult to write owing to your crowded thoughts all trying to get on to your page at once. In such a case, go back to your notes and break the topics into smaller   5.1d
ideas in a logical sequence.

If you reach a point where the words do not come easily and you cannot continue, leave the topic and start another topic or subsection. At some point your mind will clear and you can come back to finish the part that has been difficult to write.

If, however, you are writing well, but come across a small obstacle, perhaps a missing piece of information, mark that point in some way (typically a brief description of the point in square brackets) and carry on writing. Do not let a small snag interrupt you when you are in full flow.

Starting with the easiest parts of the report, i.e. the parts which you feel like writing, brings you several important advantages.

- It enables you to build up momentum from an early stage.
- It gives you some visible progress after the intangible stages of planning and information gathering, and thereby a chance to ensure that you are on the right track with your layout and style.
- It increases your morale and confidence, from which the more difficult subsections become progressively easier to write (exam technique does the same for students).
- It makes your mind more active, so that as you write, you generate further ideas.

When you complete the first draft of your first subsection, print it and review it.   5.3e

e) Appendices   Ref

As you write you will have additional ideas, most of which can be incorporated in the text, with   5.1d
occasional extra topic headings.

Sometimes you will find a demand for a lengthy diversion, such as a set of examples, a table of detail or a long explanation. As a result you often need more appendices than you had planned.

When this happens, do not waste time writing or numbering the appendices if you are concerned about losing momentum. Merely make a note of their content on your notepad and continue with writing the main text. You can index the appendices later.   5.1d

The Report Report
Notes and Observations

f) Working habits

Ref

Each person has his or her own optimum working habits, so there is little point in this report recommending how to schedule your work. The only certainty is that there will be plenty of it, so you do have to apply yourself with a degree of discipline. You therefore have to find yourself a routine (or lack of one) which enables you to produce a targeted output in each working day. And remember that five hours of high-quality work is worth more than ten hours of patchy work.

5.2g/ h

Some people's writing habits may appear bizarre, but if they work, they work. If you are writing your work in someone else's environment (e.g. your employer's) and you are finding it difficult, arrange to do your writing in a more suitable location.

g) When you're hot, you're hot

Ref

When you hit a productive spell in which you are writing rapidly and easily, don't stop ... not even if your favourite mother-in-law pays you a visit. Your best writing will usually be spontaneous, so don't waste it. Occasionally, a fertile spell produces jumbled prose from the sheer volume of thoughts, but this is usually edited easily into a smooth flow of ideas. Simply highlight the good phrases and trim out the jumbled parts (the linkage of your thoughts can be unclear when you are writing rapidly). Alternatively, you can write bullet-points and expand them into prose later.

A possible distraction is that while you are writing about one topic you find yourself thinking clearly about another one, sometimes in a different subsection. Don't fight it; go with the flow of ideas. Transfer to the other subsection and write out your ideas while your mind is active on the topic. For example, much of this subsection was written in the middle of writing the review subsection.

5.3

If all of this sounds dangerously unstructured to your orderly mind, don't worry. You have already created the structure when you set up the layout and blank subsections, so you now have the luxury of choosing the order in which you write.

5.1d

h) When you're not, you're not

Ref

There will be spells when your output slows down to the point where you can hardly think of what to write, and when you do write something you immediately delete it. There is no point in continuing at a time like this. Try writing one or two other subsections instead and if they are no better, stop writing and do something else to occupy your thoughts. When you return, make yourself a cup of coffee and, in a relaxed frame of mind, read the part you were struggling to write.

Quite often it is not as badly written as you imagined, and you can bring it up to standard with a few amendments and carry on from there. If it really is beyond rescue, then when you resume writing, do so at another subsection, or perhaps an appendix which involves figures or graphics to provide a change. After a while you will be able to return with a fresh mind to the troublesome part.

Another approach to a troublesome subsection is to write the topic headings and then fill in odd phrases or sentences of the narrative as they occur to you. You can then go back to the subsection as further points occur to you, until you can link them all together and complete it. Review any subsection completed in that manner especially carefully.

5.3e

The Report Report
Notes and Observations

THE REPORT REPORT   **5.2**
5. PRODUCTION
5.2 WRITING   Page 4 of 5

i) Rescue
                                                 Ref

If after several attempts you still cannot get part of the report right, return to the basic considerations and ask yourself if you have the fundamentals right.

- Are you writing the sections and subsections in the most logical order? (often a difficulty occurs because you are trying to write about something that has been placed too early in the report, and the introduction or explanation comes later)
- Are you using the right approach to the writing? (for example, if a narrative contains a complex jumble of related facts, it may well be easier presenting the facts in a table)   App 3D
- Is your thought process strictly correct? (for instance, are you trying to draw a conclusion which is not supported by the facts, or even at odds with them?)

If this fundamental reconsideration does not resolve the problem, enlist the help of a suitable colleague.

j) Bottlenecks
                                                 Ref

Despite the flexibility you are allowing yourself in your writing habits, you still have to manage the overall reporting process to ensure that your report is completed within the deadline. And if there is no imposed deadline, you should set yourself one or you will have great difficulty in ever finishing the report.

The main problem in managing the overall process is often bottlenecks from one or more of the following sources:

- information not yet received - a small item missing may hold up large parts of the report, particularly if there are calculations involved on which other calculations and further work depend
- work delegated to other people but not yet finished - if you are leading the project, you will be held responsible, so ensure that the people working for you keep to the schedule
- resources (computer, presentation materials, staff) not to hand - again, these are your 2.1b/c responsibility unless the client undertook in writing to provide them.

The date of completion of a report is the date of completion of the last part of it, so it is not clever to be 95% finished well before the deadline and then miss it because of something you should have pursued much earlier. You have to manage your report production as you would any other project, and the more you use other resources, especially people, the greater will be your need to plan and control ahead.

In this context, be particularly careful when the clients or addressees are providing some of the resources. It is not unknown for them to commit to providing resources which in the event fall short of the level promised, leaving you to be held responsible. Ensure that the promised resources are specified in the remit or engagement letter, and if they are not available at an early stage, request them in writing, warning of the possible delay which may result from their absence.   2.1c

Even if the client or addressees are providing staff resources of suitable quality, the staff themselves may have conflicting priorities which limit or delay their input to your report. Postponement of information-gathering interviews is a common example. If such delays start to occur to a serious extent, report them to the client immediately in a way which is sympathetic to the staff involved, and warn the client that he may be liable for additional costs or a missed deadline if additional time is taken.

The Report Report
Notes and Observations

k) Technology

Ref

The majority of narrative reporting in this age is done on word processing equipment, and if you are using this method, you should consider the following points.

Firstly, consider who is printing and publishing your report. If it is to be done on someone else's equipment, then there is no point in writing the report using software which is not compatible with theirs. Even if it is the same software, yours may be a more recent version which theirs cannot read.

Always work to the lowest common level of technology, so that your work can be transferred. If you use graphics or a special font for your reporting, ensure that it is available on the computer which will be producing the final report. Modern word-processing packages have most of the capability of desktop publishing software, so there is seldom any need to use the latter for reporting.

If you are e-mailing files of material to someone to publish, remember that they can alter it without your consent. Where security is paramount, you may have to send protected or read-only files by email, or send hard copy to avoid alteration. Remember also that many e-mail systems cannot reproduce all of the symbols available to word processing packages. £ signs and letters with accents are common examples of that.

App
5B

If you are using software, remember to apply conventional back-up disciplines. Back up frequently and ensure that your back-ups are far enough off-site to avoid a large fire, flood or crash (or earthquake in some areas). At all times there must be two up-to-date copies of the work at a safe distance from each other.

Relax and enjoy your writing - you will find that the preparation you have done is a considerable help in that direction. The more thoroughly you have completed your preparations, the more enjoyable the writing process will be.

The Report Report
Notes and Observations

The writing process is highly satisfying; at last you have a tangible product growing before your eyes. But sheets of typed paper do not a report make. To ensure that your written work reflects all your planning, you have to be carefully critical of your output from its earliest stages. Only by rigorous reviewing of your work will you produce the quality of final report which your effort (not to mention your fee to your client) deserves.

SUMMARY   Ref

These are the key considerations in the review process.

- Review the objectives and scope section at an early stage to ensure that you are heading in the right direction to meet the addressees' requirements.   5.3c
- Review the overall layout after drafting one or two subsections to ensure that the style and format with which you have started are appropriate for the whole report.   5.3d
- Review the early drafts of completed sections to ensure that the content is credible, logically sequenced and clear, and that the style is suitable.   5.3e
- If you are at all uncertain in the early stages, use a competent external reviewer.   5.3e/h
- Mark all your review points clearly in the margin of your draft.   5.3f
- As you reach an advanced draft stage with your report substantially complete, carry out a complete review of what you have written, concentrating on the logic and completeness of what you have written so far, noting omissions especially.   5.3g
- Once you have reviewed your advanced draft, have it reviewed by your external reviewer.   5.3h
- Maintain well-ordered working papers to support your points and have the papers reviewed by the external reviewer .   5.3i
- Have your final draft proof-read as well as externally reviewed.   5.3j
- If your final draft is reprinted for production, have the reprint proof-read.   5.3j

a) Objectives   Ref

The purpose of the review process is one of quality control, directed at meeting all of the client's requirements. To achieve this you must ensure that: 2.1b

- each specific requirement in the remit is fully addressed   2.1b/c
- the report as a whole reads easily, logically, consistently and understandably   3.1a
- the style and tone of the report are appropriate to the circumstances throughout   4.1a
- the report is technically and factually correct in everything it states   2.4a
- the report as a whole conveys your competence, credibility and authority

If, in addition to achieving the above objectives, your reports have a certain style which sets them above those of your competitors, that will be an additional benefit. However, do not become obsessed with your own cleverness with regard to style, or you will irritate the addressees. Critical reviewing will help you achieve this balance.

b) Approach   Ref

Although reviews all have the final objectives stated above, in practice the emphasis of the reviews changes with the following stages, which are discussed below:
- draft introduction   5.3c
- draft layout   5.3d
- early drafts   5.3e
- advanced drafts   5.3g
- final version for submission   5.3j

cont'd

The Report Report
Notes and Observations

b) Approach (continued)   Ref

You must carry out all reviews as if you were the most difficult addressee and the material had just been given to you to read without warning. It may be difficult putting yourself in this position at first, but you must keep trying until it becomes instinctive. There is not much point in your thinking that your report is excellent and his thinking that it is not what was ordered.

c) Draft introduction   Ref

When you have drafted the introduction as far as you can, ask yourself these questions.   5.2c

- Does the objectives subsection clearly set out what the remit requires, together with any additional objectives you may have?   1.1
- Does the scope subsection clearly set out the full scope of the report?   1.2
- Will fulfilment of the scope meet the objectives?   1.2
- Does the scope clearly define all the limits of the report?   1.2
- If I read this 'out of the blue', would I have a clear idea of the report's purpose?

As the introduction is only an early draft at this stage, concentrate your review on the overall direction and content which it defines, rather than on details and niceties. If you have any lingering uncertainty about the scope, direction or content, now is your last chance to contact the addressees and ask for clarification on any points.

If you clear up all your doubts in one call the addressees will approve of your attention to detail, but if you make a stream of such calls they will begin to doubt your competence. So make sure you have all your queries identified at this stage.

d) Draft layout   Ref

When you have drafted your first subsection and again when you have drafted your first whole section, review the layout you have adopted and make sure that:

- the layout and fonts are logical and pleasing to the eye   3.3-5
- the numbering system you have used is easy to understand, and able to cope with the largest subsections and sections you will be writing   3.2b-f
- the cross-reference system will be effective   3.2h
- the layout will not present any problems with filing or printing   5.2k

If you fail to carry out a layout review at this early stage you may find after drafting a large part of your report that some aspect of the layout is unsuitable, and you have to spend a lot of valuable time amending the pages you have already written. Get it right at the beginning.

If your report is likely to cross borders, bear in mind that the USA and various associated countries use letter-size paper, while the rest of the world is standardised on A4 paper. This may affect your choice of layout, or at least the way in which you set your headings and margins. No matter which paper size you use, the print will appear smaller and the margins disproportionate if your report is reproduced on the other size.

In your own interests, if your report is to appear on both paper sizes, set your layout to the paper size used by the most influential addressees.

The Report Report
Notes and Observations

e) Early drafts

Ref

Perform your reviews of your early drafting piecemeal, as the subsections and sections are completed. Ask yourself critically:

- is the order within the section or subsection logical?   3.1
- are there any gaps in the logic, and if so, how should you fill them?   3.1
- are there any topics which should be transferred to another subsection?   3.1
- is the overall style of narrative and delivery of information appropriate?   4.1-4
- is the structure of the narrative (tenses, persons etc) consistent?   4.2e-h
- is your narrative free of repeated irritations such as pet phrases, misspellings, misnomers and inaccuracies? - better to identify them and stop (mis)using them at an early stage than to have to correct the whole report   4.3
- does it instinctively "feel" right? (if not, check the above points again)

There is no optimum interval at which you should carry out early reviews. If your writing is in full flow, with ideas flowing fast, on no account should you interrupt this happy state of affairs to do a review unless you think you may be seriously adrift. But if you have doubts, print out what you have written so far, even if it is only part of a subsection, and review it critically.   5.2g

At some point you will have to have another competent person review your report. If you have any doubts at all about your work in the early stages, have that person review your early drafts even though they may only amount to a few subsections. If your approach is not appropriate, he will be able to advise you on how you need to change it.   5.3h

f) Marking your review

Ref

Unless you mark every one of your review points clearly in the margin, you will fail to make some of the necessary amendments. You may think you will pick up all of the changes when you edit the work for the next draft, but omissions are likely, as your thought process will have moved on by then.

If you mark your early reviews thoroughly, you will have much less work to do in the later stages. If you are working with someone else, ensure that you mark your review points with a marker which will be visible on the photocopy you give them for their work. Ensure also that you understand each other's marking system.

There is a comprehensive set of standard review marks used by proof-readers for book publishers, but for reports an informal system of marking will usually suffice, provided that it is simple, logical and consistent. Ensure that the person making the amendments understands the markings used.

g) Advanced drafts

Ref

As the subsections and sections are completed, you should become increasingly concerned with the way in which they knit together to form a coherent single document. The style and approach should have been established after the reviews of the first few subsections.   5.3e

cont'd

The Report Report
Notes and Observations

g) Advanced drafts (continued)   Ref

At the point where you first have a nearly complete report, however rough, print it and take time out to review it from beginning to end, imagining as always that you are a highly critical addressee. As you review the draft copy, mark on it the alterations needed and the gaps and omissions. If the alterations are too complex to mark on the draft, note them on your rough pad. This is usually necessary for structural alterations, particularly those involving changes of sequence.   5.3f

As you are reading through your report, have your original rough notes to hand and mark off the topics (do not erase them; you may wish to refer again to them) as you find them fully dealt with in the report. At the end of the review mark on your draft copy or your change notes any topics which have not yet been dealt with. Note also any outstanding information which may delay   5.1d
your report and ensure that you chase it.   5.2j

It is much more difficult to detect errors of omission than errors of commission when reviewing. It is more common to think of an omission as you are doing something else with neither laptop nor paper to hand, driving being a frequent example. After that it is a battle to try and remember it until you can write it down.   5.3h

If you make your first full review a thorough one, you will be able to bring the report to its final form much more quickly and easily.

h) Use of other reviewers   Ref

It is virtually essential to use someone else to review the pre-final and final versions of your report. But it may also be very useful to bring in an external reviewer to reinforce your review of the first full draft copy. That person should be of sufficient status and experience to be able to review the report from the point of view of the addressees.   5.3g

He will be able to review your work more critically and effectively than you can, because:

- not having written the report himself, he will read it as it has actually been written, not as the writer intended it to be written
- he will not know what the writer meant in an unclear passage, whereas the writer will already understand the intended meaning and will often fail to notice any unclear expression
- his mind will not be distracted with all of the paraphernalia of information gathering and report production
- he is more likely to notice omissions, as he will not already know the missing points in the way that the writer does and will therefore find the logic incomplete   5.3g
- he will notice your bad narrative habits and pet phrases more easily than you will   4.3

i) Working papers

Where your report is the culmination of an information-gathering process, the reviewer should examine your working papers to ensure that they fully support the findings of the report. If your findings and conclusions are likely to be called in to question, or even if you are just asked to   5.1e
provide some additional detail subsequent to submission of the report, you need to be sure that   2.3c-d
your supporting information is adequate for this purpose.

cont'd

The Report Report
Notes and Observations

i) Working papers (continued)

Ref

You may believe that you have adequately evidenced the points you have made in your report. However, it is difficult for you to review your own logic when you have already drawn your conclusions. For this reason, it is essential for an external reviewer to review the logic trail from your working documents through to the points in your report. He has not already made up his mind, and will need to be convinced in the same way that the addressees will. A diligent and intelligent external reviewer will give you a high measure of protection.

And remember, your working papers should be filed under the numbering system you have used for the report itself, to allow rapid and easy reference. Where some papers apply to more than one part of the report, file them under the number to which they relate most directly, and enter a sheet under each of the other parts to which they relate, stating the number under which they can be found. This will save considerable time on subsequent reference to the papers, especially if you have to refer to them after a long time.

3.2

j) Final version for submission

Ref

Once you are working on the report as a whole instead of individual parts of it, the emphasis of your review changes again. You should have dealt with the bulk of the errors and omissions in your first overall review, and your priority is now completion. You should be aiming to get from your first rough overall draft to your final version in as few intervening drafts as possible, although not at the expense of quality.

5.3e-g

The review process on the pre-final draft therefore focuses upon:
- any reporting matters still not dealt with (there should be few if any at this stage)
- correction of any errors from previous draft
- completeness, including all appendices and enclosures
- correctness of index numbering and cross-references (errors can occur when text is moved; every single cross-reference must be checked)
- checking of calculations - regardless of how they were prepared
- agreement of figures wherever a figure appears in more than one place
- any other details which have been omitted or incorrectly dealt with.

If the final draft is reprinted by some other process, the reprinted report will have to be proof-read. Proof-reading is not a review in that it is not critical of the content (although the proof-reader may well query anything he considers inappropriate). It is a detailed check by a competent person other than the report writer to ensure that the version of report released to the addressees matches exactly the final draft. The use of software greatly reduces the proof-reading burden, but does not eliminate errors entirely.

Be aware that if your software is set to certain defaults, it can automatically alter text after you have reviewed it. For example, the author found on several occasions that tabulated phrases which he had begun with a lower-case letter had been altered by the software to begin with an upper-case letter. He also upgraded his software half-way through this project, with the result that a number of default settings were changed and the material typed after the upgrade was presented differently from the earlier work, which had to be re-edited to achieve a consistent presentation.

Don't waste all that hard work - be sure that your final report is entirely correct before submitting it.   5.4

The Report Report
Notes and Observations

Last Chance Saloon. Be careful ... don't spoil matters by being careless at this stage. This is your ouput - the product by which people will judge you, and for which you expect them to pay you.

SUMMARY

Ref

Reports which have been painstakingly researched and carefully prepared are often compromised by hurried and careless packaging and submission. You must:

▪	establish how and when the report is to be submitted	5.4a
▪	leave sufficient time for the often complex logistics of despatch and delivery	5.4b
▪	consider involvement and prior approval by the addressees and other parties	5.4c/d
▪	consider the need for parallel summary reports	5.4e
▪	if relevant, obtain the necessary signatures properly executed	5.4f
▪	control and record distribution where confidentiality is high	5.4g
▪	provide a covering letter if practicalities and/or politics demand	5.4h
▪	ensure that the binding and packaging are as required, and adequate for the purpose.	5.4i

It may also be appropriate to present your report in person, which has to be arranged.   5.4j

If you are producing the report for a fee, you should deal with the billing promptly.   5.4k

a) Objectives

Ref

When you submit the final version of your report to the addressees, whether you hand it over or post it, that is the point of no return.

Any subsequent corrections, retractions or other amendments will compromise your integrity as a reporter and possibly as a professional in the field on which you are reporting. Even if the subsequent changes are the addressees' fault, perhaps an incorrect remit or some misinformation on their part, there will be a lingering perception that you should have identified this early on in the process.

The objectives of the submission stage are therefore to ensure that the addressees receive their report:

- in the form in which they want it (paper or disk size, binding etc)
- where they want it (correct address and confidentiality level)
- when they want it (before the deadline, not on it or after it)
- how they want it (posted, e-mailed or personally presented)
- 100% correct (with all the review and proof-reading properly completed)   5.3j
- fully supported by adequate working papers (not for presentation).   5.3i

Note that they may also want a formal oral presentation of the report.   SA1

b) Logistics

Ref

Well-prepared reports often suffer badly from hurried production and even miss their deadlines because nobody has given any attention to the logistics of copying, binding and delivering the completed report. There are many more stages than you might at first think, so be prepared for them well in advance.

cont'd

The Report Report
Notes and Observations

---

b) Logistics (continued)   **Ref**

Consider and organise the following matters long before you reach the submission date, and have all the materials and facilities ready in good time:

- time taken for approval and amendment of a draft if submitted to the addressees or any other related party   5.4c
- time taken to convert your report into another form if required (eg translation into another   5.4d
  language or software, conversion to printing on both sides or a different paper size etc)
- time, materials and equipment needed for printing, copying and binding
- preparation and inclusion of other materials (product literature, supporting documents, certificates, covering letters etc) required along with the report
- method of delivery of report to addressee
- packaging required for intact delivery (to have a well-bound document arrive at the addressees' premises battered and bent is inexcusable)
- time taken by delivery
- possible delays in delivery, including cross-border formalities
- addressees' availability around deadline date (many an addressee has demanded a report on a certain date, and been in another country throughout that week)
- preliminary sight by the addressees or another party of a draft for approval   5.4c-d
- presentation of a summary report to an associated party   5.4e
- oral presentation to addressees if required (seating, projector, material etc)   SA1
- any other factor which could prevent the report from being submitted as required

The above are all commonsense practical matters which can often be delegated to a reliable person with the relevant administration and document production skills.

c) Onward submission by addressees   **Ref**

In many cases the addressees will themselves be submitting your report onward to another party. Possible reasons are that your report is being used:

- to support a course of action which the addressees want the other party to take, or which they want to take themselves with the other party's authority
- to justify a course of action the addressees have already taken
- because the addressees have been instructed by the other party to obtain the information or advice you have provided in your report
- because a person senior to the addressees has instructed you to report to them, and wishes to have a copy of the report

In such cases, there is likely to be pressure on you to present the report in the way which is most favourable to the addressees' relations with the other party.

How far can you accommodate your addressees' wishes? You cannot report anything but what you believe to be the truth, but you may be able to express points in a manner which would help the addressees' cause without affecting the truthfulness of your report. You may also be able to include or exclude items at their request, again without affecting your truthfulness. There are no rules to cover this; you are the sole arbiter of what is the truth and what is distortion, although you can of course take advice on the subject.

cont'd

The Report Report
Notes and Observations

c) Onward submission by addressees (continued)   Ref

The best way to deal with this is usually to send the addressees your proof-read pre-final version as a draft report. Ensure that the word "draft" is stamped across the text on every page so that any unauthorised copies of pages cannot be mistaken for extracts from the final report. Send the draft to the addressees in time for them to study it so that when you meet them you can agree the final presentation of the report, or at least make such alterations as you are prepared to make.   5.3j

d) Draft submission to subject   Ref

In some cases you may have to report to addressees about a person or some aspect of a person's activities. For example, you may have to report to a bank on the viability of a business, and your report will include an assessment of the manager of that business.

In such cases it is fair and courteous, unless it has been forbidden, to show that person a proof-read pre-final version as a stamped draft, in time for you to discuss it with him before submitting it (with any resultant alterations) to the addressees. This is especially relevant if the subject of your report has helped you by providing information for the report.

This courtesy may also help you, as the subject may highlight possible improvements in your report. He will be acting as an additional reviewer, albeit very much from his own self-protective viewpoint.

There may also be occasions when you are forbidden to discuss your report with the subject. Ensure that the parameters are clearly established in writing at the outset where such sensitivities may exist.   2.1c/h

e) Split-level reporting   Ref

In some cases you may have to present two levels of report, either simultaneously or a detailed report followed by a summary report. Typically, your detailed report will be to the operational management of an organisation, and the summary report to a higher level, such as a board of directors or trustees. The summary report will be similar to the conclusions and recommendations of the main report, but is likely to be worded so that it is self-contained. Such a summary will usually be one or two pages.

All the aspects of this and other subsections apply to split-level reporting. The summary report must be as complete, reliable and clear within its own context as the main report is. The lower level of addressees will want to receive the report first.   5.4d

f) Signature   Ref

Should you sign your report or not? Many types of report legally require a signature, but many others are a matter of choice. As a general rule, it is better to sign a report, even it is informal, or a routine one-page daily format. The signature conveys to the readers that you have carried out your duty of care in preparing the report properly, and that you are prepared to stand by what you have written. If you are receiving a report, it is reassuring to see that the reporter has put his signature to it.

cont'd

f) Signature (continued)   Ref

Wherever possible, sign as few copies (the "principal copies") of the report as possible. These are usually the addressees' copies, and any other copies should have your name typed (often called "type-signed"). Even the signed copies should be type-signed, as signatures are not always easily legible. The type-signature should be exactly the same as the handwritten signature; for example, if you sign "Vladimir H Dracula" do not use a type-signature of "VH Dracula".

Photocopies are now of such high quality that it is often difficult to distinguish an original from a copy. It is therefore advisable to sign in blue ink using a fountain pen or a felt-tip pen, so that the page absorbs some ink. You should sign on a page of text (usually the last page) of the report, as signing a blank page may allow someone to insert additional text which may be assumed to be covered by your signature.

Unless there is a very good reason not to do, so, date your signature (preferably in writing). The date may be either the date from which the report is effective or the date on which it is actually signed, depending on circumstances and requirements. But be careful about back-dating or forward-dating a document by more than a short period; consider whether doing so might affect your responsibility or liability for anything you have said in the report.

It may also be necessary to initial agreed changes, and also to initial the bottom of each page of a report, depending on the circumstances. Witnesses may be needed, according to the legal status of the report and the law of the country of signature.

g) Distribution   Ref

If your report is confidential you should maintain a record of the persons to whom you send it.

If it is highly confidential, you should number each report individually and record which addressee receives each number. You should also obtain a signed confirmation from each addressee of receipt of the report. If the confidentiality level was not instructed by the addressees in the first place, their confirmation of receipt of the report should also state their understanding of the confidentiality.   2.1c/h

It may be appropriate to include the distribution list in the report itself, or in the covering letter, or merely to maintain it as a separate document. Remember that you may be asked for additional copies at a later date, and these should be subject to the same controls as the original batch unless the addressees have informed you in writing that the confidentiality restrictions have been lifted.

If your report is a regular report (for example, a monthly operations report to a management team) you will normally have a standing distribution list, usually noted at the front of the report. In such cases, you should list the addressees by the titles of their positions, whether or not their names are stated. This is because the report is for the holders of the positions rather than the individuals themselves, who may change from time to time.   SA2

The Report Report
Notes and Observations

h) Covering letter   Ref

More often than not, there are some incidental points which you wish to place on record about your report or the project as a whole, but which you do not wish to include in your report. Administrative points typically fall into this category.

The accepted way to deal with this is in a covering letter, an example of which has been included.   App
                                                                       5C

i) Binding and packaging

Ref

If the method of binding has not been specified by the client or the addresses, you have a wide choice of methods. If you consider the following points, you should be able to select the most appropriate type of binding.

- Does the client want it bound at all? (it is most irritating to receive bound documents when you want to store them in a loose-leaf file)
- How many copies are required?
- How often and over what period of time will people (not necessarily the client or the addressees) use the report? (repeated usage normally necessitates four rings if a ring-binder is used)
- How will they file the report? (for example if you are preparing inspection reports for inclusion in a client's engineering files, they may have to be bound in the client's own files, and this fact may have to be mentioned in your introductory wording)
- By what means and how often are the reports being transported?
- Do you wish to make it difficult for the reports to be photocopied?
- Do you wish to make it easy for the reports to be photocopied?
- Are the reports so confidential that they need a lockable binding?
- Do the readers wish to bind other material in with the report? (e.g. related correspondence or subsequent information)
- Is there a publicity aspect to the report, demanding a high-impact presentation?
- Will the reports be subject to any other type of special (e.g. outdoor) usage?

There are subsidiary considerations such as whether or not to have protruding tabs on the section dividers - a good idea in a hard-cover ring-binder, but less so in a soft-cover comb-binder.

The following binding methods are amongst the types commonly available:

- clips or staples, with or without soft covers
- comb-binders and other proprietary systems for use with soft covers, and allowing material to be added or removed
- proprietary systems for use with soft covers, in which the material is permanently bound and cannot be added to or removed
- ring-binders - four-ring binders are much more robust than two-ring binders, and D-rings hold the pages less destructively than O-rings
- proprietary hard-cover systems, some of them lockable (usually expensive).

Do not use lever-arch files; they distort easily. And if a third party is putting your sheets in binders, ensure the sheets are punched to your satisfaction before you hand them over; nothing is more infuriating than having someone punch your report untidily.

Finally, if you are posting files, use packaging strong enough to ensure that the reports arrive without impacted corners (very common) or other transit damage.

The Report Report
Notes and Observations

j) Presentation in person

Ref

Posting your report may be necessary as a result of distance or time constraints, but it is preferable to present your report in person, at least to the most influential of the addressees. Doing this, even briefly, offers several advantages.

- It is a courtesy which will normally be appreciated by the addressees
- It reassures the addressees of your commitment to their interests
- It enables you to deal with any sensitive issues which are not to be recorded (for example, you may have had some difficulty in dealing with one of their colleagues during the reporting process, or in obtaining promised information)

5.4c
App
5C

- It gives you a chance to warn them gently of any parts of the report likely to be unwelcome to them, and to reinforce tactfully your reasons for including these items
- It allows you to agree the methods and timescale for discussing and resolving any issues arising from the report (including the payment of your fee)
- It may enable you to identify and even confirm opportunities for further work

Some reports may require a formal oral presentation to the addressees' team.

SA1

k) Billing

Ref

If you haven't kept your records of time and costs up-to-date throughout the process, you will now wish you had, because now is the time to send out your bill for the excellent work you have done. Having to dig back through your diary and other sources means that you will probably omit to include some of the chargeable costs for the project, and suffer financially as a result.

So be sure to keep your reporting progress and cost records up to date at all times. Not only will you be able to bill the client fully, but if there are any queries regarding your costs you can answer them promptly, providing any necessary evidence.

Congratulations: you have given birth to a high-quality product. But inmixed with your pride and satisfaction is a mild form of post-natal depression... your adrenalin has disappeared, you feel flat and strangely unmotivated, and you certainly cannot face the pile which has accumulated in your in-tray while you have been working flat-out on the report.

So go and take your reporting team out for a couple of drinks, have a good laugh about the things that went wrong during the project, and return tomorrow ready for anything.

The Report Report
Notes and Observations

The lines show the blank format of the layout of the text of this report, which was prepared largely in MS Word, with occasional pages in MS Excel. (This actual book is compiled from the original MS documents, re-cast in QuarkXpress, a universally accepted program for book production.) The borders are hidden from the reader.

a)	Heading	Ref
	Text	

b)	Heading	Ref
	Text	

c)	Heading	Ref
	Text	

d)	Heading	Ref
	Text	

The Report Report
Notes and Observations

5B ACCENTS AND SYMBOLS

When using non-English words you are likely to need accents on letters. With Microsoft software, these can be typed by holding down the Alt key and simultaneously pressing certain numbers on the keyboard number pad. For example, Alt+130 gives you é.

You can also type other useful symbols using this facility. Alt+157 gives you ¥ and Alt+156 produces £, essential if you are using a non-British PC which does not have a £ key. The □uro symbol is Alt+0128, but you may need to load special software to produce it. To obtain this, contact your software provider.

Note that this does not work with the row of number keys along the top of the keyboard. So if you are using a laptop, you will have to put it into number pad mode to use this facility. The range of accents and symbols is set out below. It varies slightly with different versions of software.

	0	1	2	3	4	5	6	7	8	9
Alt + 1	□					¤				
Alt + 2	¶	§								
Alt + 3			space	!	"	#	$	%	&	'
Alt + 4	(	)	*	+	,	-	.	/	0	1
Alt + 5	2	3	4	5	6	7	8	9	:	;
Alt + 6	<	=	>	?	@	A	B	C	D	E
Alt + 7	F	G	H	I	J	K	L	M	N	O
Alt + 8	P	Q	R	S	T	U	V	W	X	Y
Alt + 9	Z	[	\	]	^	_	`	a	b	c
Alt + 10	d	e	f	g	h	i	j	k	l	m
Alt + 11	n	o	p	q	r	s	t	u	v	w
Alt + 12	x	y	z	{			}	~	□	Ç	ü
Alt + 13	é	â	ä	à	å	ç	ê	ë	è	ï
Alt + 14	î	ì	Ä	Å	É	æ	Æ	ô	ö	ò
Alt + 15	û	ù	ÿ	Ö	Ü	¢	£	¥	P	ƒ
Alt + 16	á	í	ó	ú	ñ	Ñ	ª	º	¿	
Alt + 17	¬	½	¼	¡	«	»	_			¦
Alt + 18										
Alt + 19										
Alt + 20										
Alt + 21										
Alt + 22						ß				
Alt + 23	µ									
Alt + 24		±				·	÷		°	•
Alt + 25			²							

The easiest way to use this table is to make a smaller table in alphabetical order of the accents you need for the language you are using, and then tape the small table below your PC screen. Remember that many languages use accents, and that the spelling you are used to seeing may have the accents removed. Examples are Reykjavík and Sinn Féin, neither of which you might expect to have an accent.

Some letter fonts also make it possible to produce Cyrillic lettering on a standard keyboard.

Caution: Before using these symbols, make sure other software can understand them. For instance, if you use the word 'café' in e-mail, it may display it as 'caf'. So in such cases just write 'cafe' without the acute accent.

The Report Report
Notes and Observations

As noted in 5.4h, a covering letter is useful to deal with points which you do not consider appropriate for inclusion in your report, but which nevertheless need to be brought to the attention of the addressees. Or it may just be a short note for the sake of courtesy, which seldom goes amiss.

Operations Director
Client Civil Engineering

RE Porter
Address
Date

STRICTLY CONFIDENTIAL - ADDRESSEE ONLY

Dear Shelagh

MEKON INSTALLATIONS - HEALTH INSPECTION

I have pleasure in enclosing four copies of my signed report on the potential health hazards arising from the Mekon installations. You will be pleased to note that apart from the emission problems at the W13 and K35 sites, there are no areas of serious concern, although a number of minor items will necessitate additional procedures in your routine maintenance programmes.

Once you have discussed the report with your maintenance team, we should meet to resolve any consequent queries and actions. I shall then be in a position to release copies of the report to Megalith Insurance as instructed. The deadline for their receipt of the report is the 17th, so we need to have your response to the report cleared by the 12th to have the documents ready for despatch. Please let me know by return if you see any problem in meeting these dates.

The cooperation we received from your site management, with one exception noted below, was willing and effective, and I should be grateful if you would convey the thanks of our inspection teams to your field managers for their hard work on our behalf and their helpful attitude.

Regrettably, we had difficulty in gaining access to the sites in Q sector. Despite our early written clearance requests, copies of which are attached, we did not gain access until two weeks after the scheduled dates. Thanks to cooperation from K sector, we were able to reduce the delay by rescheduling some work on their sites, but we still incurred additional costs for delay and rearranged travel and accommodation. Had this been a minor problem I would have ignored it but, as you will see from the enclosed schedule, the costs were substantial and I shall have to present an additional bill.

However, I hope that this isolated incident will not detract from what I believe has been a valuable exercise, and I hope that we shall have the opportunity to work together on future projects.

I look forward to hearing from you once you have discussed the report with your maintenance team.

Yours sincerely
RE Porter

Note that the covering letter:

- *is written in professional language which is nevertheless not too formal, suggesting a well-established working relationship between the reporter and the client*
- *meets difficulties head-on, but in a matter-of-fact and non-political way, without any suggestion of personal grievance*
- *drives the client towards completion of the project (although it is the client who calls the tune, it is always necessary to ensure that the client does not impede the process, and this can call for diplomacy on occasion)*
- *emphasises the reporter's desire for further work for the client (in practice, this would probably be expressed once the reports had been discussed and the consequent matters dealt with).*

The Report Report
Notes and Observations

SPECIAL APPLICATIONS

SA1 ORAL PRESENTATIONS

a   Objectives
b   Principles
c   Layout
d   Speaking style
e   Personality
f   Presentation - the WRONG way
g   Presentation - the RIGHT way

APPENDIX

SA1-A Examples of slides for projection

SA2 ROUTINE REPORTING

a   Objectives
b   Initiating a routine report
c   Content
d   Layout
e   Style
f   Production

APPENDICES

SA2-A Example of weekly report
SA2-B Example of management minute

THE REPORT REPORT

An oral presentation can be a double-edged weapon. On the one hand it gives you the opportunity to argue your points and convince any sceptics of your sound reasoning. On the other hand you will have to answer questions without recourse to your working notes if you are to be convincing. If you have done your preparation, you will enjoy your presentation once you are in full swing.

SUMMARY

Ref

The objectives of an oral presentation are the same as the objectives of a written report - give your audience the information they want ... clearly, logically and convincingly.

To do this, keep it simple, low-key and use the following approach:

▪ design your talk as you would a written report - your section, subsection and topic headings become your slide headings and points	SA1c
▪ keep your slides simple, with large print	SA1-A
▪ check your location and facilities beforehand	SA1g
▪ speak in a relaxed manner, friendly but respectful, clear and concise - don't hurry	SA1d/e
▪ smile - they don't know what you feel like inside	SA1e/g
▪ maintain eye-contact with your audience individually and involve them by asking questions from time to time	SA1e
▪ avoid giving your audience notes or slides to read while you are talking	SA1g
▪ repeat any important points for emphasis	SA1g

a) Objectives

Ref

You may have to present your report in oral form in addition to (or even instead of) presenting it in written form. If the addressees ask you to do this, it is usually for several reasons.

▪ It is a more comfortable way to receive the information initially.

▪ Your talk will be in summary form, leaving them to peruse the written detail at their own speed.

▪ They can gauge the extent of your conviction regarding the points you make.

▪ They can question you as points arise.

▪ They can discuss your points amongst themselves as they hear them - this clarifies issues at the earliest possible stage, and also speeds up any subsequent decisions arising from the report.

▪ When they do read the written report, it will be easier to assimilate (this is normally an advantage to you as well).

Occasionally the addressees may require an oral presentation after they have read the report. This is easier for you in that they will be already familiar with the content, but they will also have thought about it and discussed it, so be prepared for much sharper questioning.

Those are the objectives of the addressees in having an oral presentation. Your own objectives are the same as they are for the written report: give them what they have asked for, clearly and convincingly.

The Report Report
Notes and Observations

b) Principles

Ref

The principles of preparing and presenting a talk are exactly the same as the principles of written reporting. However, there are two main additional factors:

- how do you present the information visually in summarised form?

- how do you deliver the information with maximum impact in spoken form?

c) Layout

Ref

If your oral presentation is in addition to your written report, then you have dealt with the layout already. Your information has been carefully ordered in the right sequence for the addressees (your audience) to hear logically, building on their knowledge as you proceed. Your section, subsection and item headings are effectively your guidance notes for your talk, and also your slides if you are using some form of projection on a screen.

If on the other hand your report is to be presented orally without the accompaniment of a written report, you should lay out your information in the sequence which you would use if you were presenting a written report.

In practice, even if you are not presenting a formal report with your talk, you will usually have to provide your audience with a set of notes to take away afterwards. Those notes are effectively   5.1b a report, even if they are merely in note format. Some speakers simply provide written copies of their projected slides (occasionally with space for the audience to add their own notes).

When you designed the report, you listed the main section and subsection headings and topics on a notepad. This process gives you the content and framework of your talk, and if you are using   5.1b slides for projection, it virtually designs your slides for you.

- Your first slide is an index of the main sections of your report, and it allows you to outline SA1-A what you are going to be telling your audience.

- Your second slide is the index to the first section - again, you outline what you will be SA1-A covering, each item on the slide being the heading of a subsection.

- Your next slide bears the heading of the first subsection, and will look like an abbreviated SA1-A version of the summary in bold print at the beginning of each subsection of this report - this gives you the individual topics and points you will want to cover.

- You may also wish to interject diagrams and other detailed slides at times to illustrate your points - these slides correspond roughly to the appendices you would have in a written report.

Setting up your slides is therefore equivalent to setting up your report index, down to topic level. The notes on presentation technique tell you how best to present the slides, and how not to do it.   SA1h

d) Speaking style

The considerations governing what style of talk to give are exactly the same as those governing what style of writing you would use. However, in an oral presentation you have the luxury of being able to watch your audience's reactions and adjust your style as you proceed. Regardless of who the audience are and what their culture is, you must speak slowly - at a relaxed pace, but not ponderously.

cont'd

The Report Report
Notes and Observations

d) Speaking style (continued)   Ref

You must consider carefully the audience you will be addressing and in particular:

- their status   4.1c
- their political and personal sensitivities   4.1d
- their objectives and expectations   2.2d
- their collective culture   4.1b
- their understanding of your language (even if they are English speakers, it may be a very different English from yours).

There are, however, some general differences in style between reporting in writing about a subject and talking about it. Firstly, the advantages of talking:

- Even at the highest levels of audience, you can be slightly less formal and more colloquial when speaking than you would be in writing - what sounds quite natural in a written report may sound pompous if spoken in the same words.
- You have the added benefit of using your voice, facial expression and gestures to complement your words; this gives you the ability to give much better emphasis to the important points.
- There is less risk in using occasional humour, but ensure that it is relevant and understated;   4.1f
  do not tell anecdotes or stories unless they are closely related to your subject, but rely instead on spontaneous humour if possible.
- You can dominate the proceedings, even when speaking to a senior audience, but it takes skill and experience to do that - don't push your luck.

Secondly, the disadvantages of talking:

- You have to ensure that your speech is both clear enough (i.e. slow enough) to be understood and loud enough to be heard - always speak to the back row.
- You are not always able to influence the location, time and facilities where you are giving your talk - you should try to check these beforehand or you may find yourself shouting above background noise to an audience full of lunch, and you will be unable to impart any style at all.

If you are speaking to people from other areas, remember that you have an accent, even if you think you don't. People from quick-speaking areas such as London, Glasgow and Dublin have to work much harder to be understood clearly than people from slow-speaking areas such as Yorkshire, the Scottish Highlands and Australia. People who learn English thoroughly as a second language are generally the clearest English speakers of all, the Dutch being a prime example.

Although you may use less formal language when talking, you still have to use clear,   4.4
grammatical English. You should purge your everyday speech of the less attractive
colloquialisms, including the following:

- meaningless fillers - *obviously, to be honest, the fact is, having said that* etc   4.3n
- vagueness - *sort of, kind of, you know* etc   4.3n
- current clichés, except when used ironically (if your audience understands irony).   4.3c

Without sounding as if you have just come from elocution classes, speak fairly slowly, giving slight emphasis to the important words.

- *In the **desert** we have equipped the **stealth units** with **fast** support transport, so their supplies can be delivered at **short** notice, on **time**, to the **right** location.*

Avoid emphasising prepositions, or you will sound like a third-rate 1960s disc jockey.

- ***In** the desert we have equipped the stealth units **with** fast support transport, so their supplies can be delivered **at** short notice, **on** time, **to** the right location [**with** the latest hits, **on** your favourite station, **in** the midnight hour].*

The Report Report
Notes and Observations

e) Personality

Ref

Everyone has a different personality, and you should not try to be something or someone you patently are not. However, you should use your best efforts to make your audience receptive to you as a person; if they like and respect you, they are more likely to feel the same about what you have to say to them.

Here are a few things you should do whatever kind of personality you have.

- Appear relaxed, even if you do not feel so, and even if the subject is very serious.
- Be quietly authoritative, but approachable - the two are fully compatible, and being unapproachable is a sure sign of personal insecurity.
- Unless it is clearly inappropriate, smile - not with your teeth, but with your eyes, your words and your gestures.
- Maintain eye contact with all of your audience - look at them individually, and don't let them opt out.
- Be courteous, especially when you are disagreeing with a member of the audience, but do not be obsequious.
- Be mobile in a relaxed way - don't fidget or barge about.

If you achieve the above, you will appear to be in control.

f) Presentation - the WRONG way

Ref

As the human mind learns 80% from sight, it is almost essential to have a display in note form to summarise your points. In the majority of cases, these visual aids are presented ineffectively, even by experienced people who should know better.

- The print is too small, especially on the graphics.   SA1A
- The points are not consistently presented.   SA1A
- The audience do not have a clear view of the screen.
- The presenter has the notes on the screen while he is speaking, thereby losing the audience's attention immediately.   SA1g
- The presenter does little more than read out the notes, which the audience have already read mentally before thinking about something else.   SA1g
- The presenter talks to the screen, with his back to the audience (guaranteeing that his shirt is not tucked in).   SA1g
- The presenter leaves the notes on the screen and starts talking about something else, effectively splitting the audience's attention, if he has not already lost it.   SA1g

g) Presentation - the RIGHT way

Ref

You cannot afford to ruin days, weeks or months of work with a shoddy presentation. Given that most presentations are of a low standard, you have an opportunity to differentiate yourself positively from your competition by following a few simple rules. Here they are.

If you are using software to present your visual displays, e-mail or post it to the addressees' location beforehand, so that it is their responsibility to have it working. We now have technology which can delay us for an hour while someone tries to persuade a reluctant laptop to read a presentation diskette brought by a visiting speaker who is ostensibly using the same software. If you are lucky enough to be using a traditional overhead projector, ensure beforehand that is set up and working, and that a tested spare bulb is to hand.

cont'd

The Report Report
Notes and Observations

g) Presentation - the RIGHT way (continued)   **Ref**

Then on with the presentation. Notes on designing slides are given at the back of this section. SA1A
This is how best to use them.

- Ensure that the minimum height of print used in your slides is 15mm on the page, and that
  includes graphics, the print on which is almost always invisible to the audience (small rooms
  need big lettering because the projector is closer to the screen, and big rooms also need big
  lettering because the seats are further away).
- Place your next slide on a white background in front of you, but **not on the screen**.
- Because your slide is in large letters, you can see it from a distance, so walk about in a
  relaxed way and **talk to your audience**, looking at them individually - you can always glance SA1e
  back at your slide, but you are not slavishly reading from it.
- Ask your audience questions in a non-threatening way - you know most of the answers from SA1e
  your research, but it gets them participating and helps break down any you-and-them
  barriers.
- When you have finished the topic of your slide, show the slide on the screen, summarise the
  points with appropriate emphasis and ask for any questions - if you don't know the answer
  to a question, say so - don't try and bluff.
- While they are doing this, put your next slide on the table and use it to collect your thoughts
  on the next topic - don't be afraid to have a short, reflective silence.
- Check that the audience have assimilated the previous slide, remove it and regain their attention
  for the next topic - they have nothing else to look at but you, and you are in control.

Do not give out any notes to your audience until after you have finished. Why should they listen
to you talking when they have it all written down in front of them?

Not too difficult, is it? Unfortunately, 90% of presenters will continue mumbling to the tiny print
on their screen. It is more comfortable than facing an audience.

Make sure you are one of the ten per cent who delivers the message to the audience.

The other big factor is time; a high percentage of speakers overrun their allotted time and do not
make any friends in the process. The way to get this right is to do one or two full rehearsals of
your talk in front of a colleague or a mirror. Time yourself, make the necessary adjustments and
mark the times at which you should be finishing each section - not the time on the clock (the
speaker before you will have overrun) but the number of minutes until your finishing time.
Remember to leave time for questions.

When you start speaking, take your watch off and place it by your notes so that it is always visible
and you can glance at it without making it obvious. Set the bezel on your watch so that you are
working **towards** zero, e.g. starting at 15 if you are doing a 45 minute talk, so that the watch
always tells you how much time you have left. If the incompetence of the organisers or a previous
speaker has left you with a shortened time, it may be worth taking twenty seconds to remark the
times on your notes and adjust your bezel accordingly; the audience will allow you a short period
to set your stage.

When you are ready, smile as you introduce yourself and keep on smiling. Not a fixed rictus, but
a relaxed expression which says that you are in control.

As with most other aspects of the report, think always about your audience and keep it simple.

The Report Report
Notes and Observations

A few simple rules for designing slides to support your presentation (examples below):

- use a large print - at least 15mm high when on an A4 transparency (that includes graphics)
- keep the slides simple - the rule of fives recommends no more than five points
- keep each point simple - half a dozen words or fewer
- keep the points on each slide homogeneous - all commands or all statements or all questions or all adjectives or whatever, but not a mix of nouns, verbs, questions etc
- forget about distracting visual effects - use simple strong lettering on a plain contrasting background

1. The following slide introduces
an oral presentation of this report
and should be on screen as you begin

2. This slide introduces your subject,
and should be on screen
after you have outlined your talk

THE
REPORT REPORT

RE Porter
Date

THE REPORT REPORT
1.   Introduction
2.   Content
3.   Layout
4.   Style
5.   Production
Special applications

---

3. This introduces the production section
and should be on screen
after you have outlined the section

4. This introduces the design subsection
and should be on screen
after you have outlined the subsection

---

5. PRODUCTION
5.1   Design
5.2   Writing
5.3   Review
5.4   Submission

5.1 DESIGN
a   Objectives
b   Overall content
c   Indexing
d   Detailed content
e   Information gathering
f   Blank format (template)

---

5. The "writing" subsection is a long one
and should be split into two slides,
breaking at the most logical point

6. Each part of this subsection slide
should be on the screen
after you have finished the last point

5.2 WRITING (1)
a   Objective
b   Style
c   Introduction
d   Main content
e   Appendices

5.2 WRITING (2)
f   Working habits
g   Productive spells
h   Unproductive spells
I   Bottlenecks
j   Technology

As you can see, the structure is the same as that of your written report. Notice that you don't need to include the "summary" topic in each subsection, as you will be summarising the topics yourself. Your whole talk is a summary - you will not be going into as much detail as the written report. The logic, however, follows that of the report throughout your talk.

The Report Report
Notes and Observations

The majority of reports are not individually commissioned - they are routine reports, submitted against defined timetables or on the occurrence of specified events. Examples are:

- *military, police or scientific surveillance reports*
- *a contractor's daily report to his client*
- *daily, weekly, monthly, quarterly or annual management reports in a business.*

SUMMARY
          Ref

Routine reports have the same objectives as other reports: to inform in a way that stimulates appropriate action. The only differences in reporting are in emphasis.   SA2a

- Objectives, scope, content, addressee status and similar considerations are defined when the report is initiated and do not have to be restated.   SA2b
- Content may be restricted by the need for speed, provided that accuracy is sufficient for decision-making.   SA2c
- Layout and style are condensed, as addressees are familiar with the topics.   SA2 d/e
- Report production is geared towards speed, provided again that accuracy is sufficient for decision-making.   SA2f
- The key to rapid production of reports is to ensure that information is collected and processed in the appropriate format from the beginning.   SA2f

Examples of a weekly company performance report and a minute of a weekly management meeting are at the back of this section.   SA2-A / SA2-B

a) Objectives
          Ref

The objectives of routine reports are the same as the objectives of any other reports. However, they are part of an overall operating framework, and we must therefore consider them in that context if we are to design and write effective routine reports.   1.1

It has often been pointed out that management is a cycle involving the following steps, which have to be clearly defined and followed for management to be effective:

- someone carries out an **action** - this can be a single specific action such as a product upgrade, or a routine repetitive action such as working on a production line
- someone takes a **measurement** of that action - a single action can have many aspects to measure, such as quantity, speed, success rate, rejection rate, manpower, material, cost, sales value etc
- someone makes an **analysis** of the measurement - measurements are seldom meaningful unless they are compared with relevant benchmarks such as targets, standards, previous periods, other departments, best-ever achievements etc   3.4i
- someone presents a **report** of that analysis to the management - as we have seen, an effective report distils the analysis into summarised findings with conclusions and recommendations
- the management instructs a further **action** - the instruction may be merely to continue acting as before, or it may be to act specifically to deal with a factor highlit by the report (positive factors should be exploited and adverse factors remedied)

The above cycle is probably demonstrated most clearly by the classic manufacturing process, which gives rise to detailed production figures which go through the distillation described above in time for a weekly production meeting. It is apparent that all of the methods we have discussed in the previous sections must apply to the above cycle, so why do routine reports look so different from this report?   SA2b

The Report Report
Notes and Observations

b) Initiating a routine report

When a manager, commander or other leader initiates a routine report, he must specify the following details to the person designing and/or preparing the report:

	Ref
• objectives of the report	1.1
• the persons who are to receive the report, and the timetable	1.1
• the scope and content of the report - coverage, accuracy, units and other details (designing a mandatory format often helps to ensure compliance)	1.2
• the layout of the report - sometimes precisely, especially if a format is set	
• the style of the report - this is seldom specified in words, but the combination of the subject, timetable, content and format usually dictate the style	

In initiating the report the manager has therefore taken care of much of the process before the first report has been started, thereby saving a considerable amount of time.   1.1-2

Hence routine reports tend not to have any introduction. The introduction has already been defined, and only the title of the report is needed. It is good practice to begin the report with a list of the persons (preferably by job title) to whom the report is to be distributed, but even that is not necessary in many cases, particularly in smaller organisations. The initiator should carry out a regular review of the distribution list; it is common for a person to continue receiving a routine report for years after it has ceased to have any relevance to him.

c) Content

Reports are about the future. Even though they consist largely of historical data, they are usually written with the purpose of stimulating and controlling action. The most effective content is therefore that which will best stimulate the most appropriate action.   SA2a

The shorter the interval between reports, the shorter the report should normally be, for two reasons:

- if a long report has to be written frequently, it becomes a chore to the writer and rapidly loses impact through being unenthusiastically and even sloppily prepared
- similarly, it becomes a burden to the addressees, who spend too much time in reading reports and not enough in taking action   SA2a

Accuracy will vary according to the subject matter. Some figures, such as units of product produced by a factory, can be measured accurately, while others, especially those which depend on external input, have to be estimated. Where local reports are being collated into a larger overall report, you will have to set a degree of detail which is appropriate for both the individual reports and the overall report.

There is often a trade-off between accuracy and speed. In a frequent (e.g. weekly) report, the main objective is to keep the management apprised (as opposed to appraised!) of the current situation and of the actions they need to take. Where detail takes time to acquire, it is therefore often better to make an educated estimate. This may be a little inaccurate in the first few reports, but report-writers quickly devise methods of making increasingly accurate estimates.   App 4B

In a less frequent (e.g. monthly) report, accuracy becomes more essential, as the addressees expect the report to be comprehensive and usually study it at greater length. Thus there may be a slightly longer production time needed for the report.   SA2f

cont'd

The Report Report
Notes and Observations

c) Content (continued)   Ref

Figures lend themselves easily to a standard format, but many reports are highly narrative in content. For example, if you are a company director, you may have to submit a monthly narrative report to the board of directors to supplement the statistics you provide. A routine narrative report should ideally have a standard set of headings to ensure that essential ongoing topics are covered in each report.

The drawback of this is that the narrative becomes stilted and perfunctory. You should therefore vary the emphasis within the headings from period to period. For example, In one report you can raise detailed concerns about your distributor network, and in the next give close consideration to product pricing, and so on. Where targeting is part of your reporting environment, your narrative should cover your strategy, tactics and actions towards attaining your targets. It should explain your figures, not repeat them.   SA2-B

d) Layout

All of the layout considerations discussed in this report apply just as much to short routine   3.1-5
reports as they do to major single reports.

The difference is that routine reports are more condensed in layout. Since they are being presented to addressees whose status, knowledge and culture is already fully understood, there is much less need for explanation. Routine reports therefore concentrate on presenting a lot of data in a small space, with abbreviated terms to describe familiar situations.

Familiarity is both the strength and the danger. It gives the addressees instant access to what they want to know, but as time passes, they become less diligent in their reading of the reports, and therefore less inclined to detect the need for action.   SA2a

It is therefore effective psychology to change (and improve, if possible) the format of routine reports two or three times a year. This does not entail a major redraft, but minor alterations such as the addition of new sections which have become relevant and the removal of sections which are no longer important. There may also be temporary circumstances which should be reported for a while until they have been dealt with, after which they can be removed from the report.

In this way you can have the benefit of a familiar reporting system, while still keeping the readers alert to the changing circumstances the organisation.

e) Style   Ref

In routine reports the writing style, like the layout, should be condensed.

The best example is the minutes of a meeting. In the minutes of an annual general meeting the secretary records who proposed motions, who seconded them, how many people voted for them and all kinds of excruciating detail, sometimes including arguments in a discussion. By contrast, the minutes of a weekly management meeting should ignore all of that, and only record items relating to the future:

- the precise actions which have been agreed   SA2B
- who on the management team is responsible for having the actions taken   SA2B
- the date by which the actions are to be completed   SA2B

The minutes will not take long to complete, and are therefore likely to be accurate, timely and to the point. They are a satisfying document to produce, as they serve a visible and direct action list for driving the organisation towards its goals.

The Report Report
Notes and Observations

f) Production

Ref

Production of frequent routine reports has a different emphasis from production of a single major report. While the constraints of quality and especially accuracy still apply as far as is practicable, the overriding requirement is one of speed.

5.1-4

To put this in perspective, if you are writing a report on the previous week's activities and you deliver it to the addressees first thing on Tuesday morning, you have already missed 20% of the current week's activities, for which it is too late to take any action.

SA2-B

Many UK companies who regard themselves as effectively managed have their monthly board meetings around the 20th of each month. The directors receive copies of the previous months' management accounts, together with associated narrative reports, by about the 15th of the month, which gives the directors time to read the reports in time to be prepared for the meeting.

This is ponderously slow. If there are problems in October, November's results will already be well and truly down the pan before any remedial actions are agreed. No action will be taken in December because everyone is winding down for Christmas, and in January they will be too busy getting the business back on its feet after the holidays. By the February board meeting the directors have forgotten the details of the problem; the whole matter is reconsidered and action finally begins to bite in March.

There are twenty-two working days in the average month. You should have the monthly performance reports issued, digested and discussed and actions instructed by the end of the third working day of the following month, which means that you will only lose about 15% of the month with regard to your action points. Even that can hurt.

Speed is king. With the computerised recording and reporting systems available today there is little if any excuse for any organisation not having its weekly and monthly reports produced within a short time, to a degree of accuracy which is enough to enable appropriate actions. In the USA, some national retail organisations know the daily operating results of every branch within half an hour of close of business.

The real key to speed of report production is not in the production process itself. Instead, you have to go right back to the beginning of the information recording system and ensure that the information is collected and presented in such a way that it arrives on your desk in the exact format required by your report. The more careful the design you do upstream, the less panic you will have downstream (that should be obvious, but while people usually apply that principle to technical processes, they ignore it inexplicably often in reporting processes).

Some routine reports are collected merely for long-term analysis, and these are not subject to such stringent parameters. They are, however, the exception.

Routine reports follow the principles of major reports. All that differs is the emphasis and level of detail.

The Report Report
Notes and Observations

The report shown on page 2 is a weekly report similar to that used by a number of companies, especially those which are part of a group. The report is primarily financial, but even if you are not a financial person, study the report to see how much information it manages to display on one page, and how it points the management team towards their targets. You can easily use this approach for other fields of work. In accordance with international convention, negative figures are in brackets.

Columns - the report is for the five-week "month" of October 200X (August and September were four-week months, in which the fifth column was blank) and the totals for the month are compared with the budgeted amounts set before the financial year began

Progress - the first two weeks have passed, and the columns are headed "estimate" as they contain estimated figures to date (fairly accurately estimated, as it happens), while the remaining three columns are headed "target" since they contain the figures expected of the management team

Orders - the opening orders show that the company is behind its budgeted order book of 300, and the 100 per week for the last three weeks is intended to bring it swiftly back on track (many companies have a habit of despatching a high percentage of their sales in the final week of each month, a habit called "back-end loading" which causes a variety of insidious management and financial problems)

Trading results - the despatches figure in the orders forecast creates the sales figures in the results forecast, followed by the expected margins and operating costs (note that the business has trimmed its overhead levels to compensate for its sales being below budget but that its result is worsened by a non-recurring cost, shown separately in order not to distort the underlying performance)

Receivables - the balances due by customers will be increased by the sales value (plus VAT) and reduced by the cash received (see "risk debts" below)

Payables - the same applies in the other direction to suppliers, who expect to be paid on time if they are to continue to supply materials and services

Cash - this table accounts for the targeted receipts from customers and payments to suppliers, together with any other transactions (payroll, taxes and lease instalments being the big ones), and the balance must be kept within the company's overdraft limit

Risk debts - major receivables which are overdue are highlit to ensure that management continues to pursue them for the cash, and that any disputes (eg faulty products) delaying the collection are resolved quickly, since the longer the debts remain outstanding, the harder they become to collect

Personnel - management must ensure that the personnel resources are adequate but not excessive for the company's projected level of activity

Projects - technical projects have a tendency to overrun, and the manager responsible for projects must be held to his commitments regarding completion dates and costs (if he does not report regularly on their projects, the rest of the management team lose track of the progress of the projects, which overrun and fail to meet customer and financial constraints)

Implementation - this report was distributed on the morning of Monday 13 October to the management team, who instructed the necessary actions and reported to the CEO at the weekly meeting first thing on Tuesday morning

Outcome - this simple sheet contains much key information, and causes the management team to concentrate relentlessly on the task ahead. Only two hours of each Monday morning are taken in producing the report - the actions are initiated on Monday afternoon and reported at a management meeting held first thing on Tuesday. It is effective routine reporting, devised by an accountant.

The Report Report
Notes and Observations

UK£000	Estimate 3-Oct	Estimate 10-Oct	Target 17-Oct	Target 24-Oct	Target 31-Oct	Forecast	Budget	Variance
						TOTAL FOR MONTH		
Opening orders	262	308	288	278	278	**262**	300	(38)
Orders received	66	38	100	100	100	**404**	382	22
Orders despatched	(20)	(58)	(110)	(100)	(100)	**(388)**	(382)	(6)
Closing orders	308	288	278	278	278	**278**	300	(22)
Sales	20	58	110	100	100	**388**	382	(6)
Est value added	55%	58%	58%	56%	56%	**57%**	54%	3%
	11	34	64	56	56	**221**	205	16
Labour & overheads	(37)	(37)	(37)	(37)	(37)	**(185)**	(197)	12
Non-recurring	0	0	0	(7)	0	**(7)**	0	(7)
Result before tax	(26)	(3)	27	12	19	**29**	8	21
Opening receivables	425	369	395	469	463	**425**	439	(14)
Sales	20	58	110	100	100	**388**	382	6
VAT	0	0	2	2	2	**6**	0	6
Cash receipts	(76)	(32)	(38)	(108)	(66)	**(320)**	(309)	11
Closing receivables	369	395	469	463	499	**499**	512	(13)
Opening payables	(470)	(462)	(468)	(494)	(505)	**(470)**		
Purchases	(43)	(50)	(50)	(50)	(30)	**(223)**		
VAT	(4)	(5)	(6)	(6)	(4)	**(25)**		
Payments	55	49	30	45	45	**224**		
Closing payables	(462)	(468)	(494)	(505)	(494)	**(494)**	(405)	(89)
Opening cash	(335)	(326)	(338)	(334)	(362)	**(335)**	(447)	112
Receipts - custmrs	76	32	38	108	66	**320**		
Receipts - other	0	22	0	0	0	**22**		
Payments - supplrs	(55)	(49)	(30)	(45)	(45)	**(224)**		
Payments - other	(12)	(17)	(4)	(91)	(22)	**(146)**		
Closing cash	(326)	(338)	(334)	(362)	(363)	**(363)**	(465)	102

Risk debts	Total	Current	30 days	60 days	90 days	Comments
Andersson	33	0	8	4	21	agreed payment by 15 Dec
Claritec	41	3	19	0	19	awaiting replacement Kappa
Miklas	30	8	0	0	22	paying 10 per month
SSP Orient	13	0	0	0	13	still claiming defect
Wentworth	16	0	0	16	0	meeting this week
Other receivables	366	249	91	5	21	
Total receivables	499	260	118	25	96	

	Prodn	Control	Selling	Admin	R & D	Staff		
Personnel number	17	13	14	9	12	**65**	72	-7

Major projects		Start	Finish	Stage	Budget	Estimate	Comments
Kappa		Jan-0X	Dec-0X	95%	67	58	mods now under test
Epsilon	US cert	Jun-0X	Jan-0Y	60%	74	92	lab report imminent
	adaptor	May-0X	Noc-0X	80%	10	7	safety clearance requested
	NT	Nov-0W	Dec-0X	90%	23	25	HBN delivering end Oct
	Berlin	Apr-0X	May 0Z	10%	24	?	no spec from Berlin - chase
Mark 5	casing	Aug-0X	?	25%	62	?	reactivate?

The Report Report
Notes and Observations

The example of a minute on page 2 (page 2 of this appendix, but page 1 of the minute) shows a format which the author has found effective for company management.

Objectives - *management minutes are part of the management cycle discussed in SA2a, and are intended to drive the actions agreed by the managers from their analysis of the information reaching them through the cycle.*

Content - *statutory minutes (e.g. shareholders' and directors' minutes) are heavy going, comprising formal accounts of motions presented, arguments put forward, people's views to be put on record, documents approved and so on, but management minutes should be almost entirely about action - only the occasional satisfactory feedback note will not need an action.*

Length - *ideally the minutes should be restricted to one page, but in young companies, especially technology companies, management meetings tend to be over-detailed and minutes run to one and a half pages - if they extend to two pages the team is getting bogged down in matters which should be delegated to subordinates (managers in young companies have to make a special effort to develop themselves and their subordinates to the point where all non-management work is delegated).*

Sections - *unlike a statutory minute, a management minute does not have to be chronological, so the action notes can be grouped into areas of interest or responsibility, resulting in a more easily readable document and greater likelihood of the actions being implemented without omission.*

Dates - *every action minuted should carry a completion date, or the action will languish - "immed" means immediately after the meeting, but ASAP is a nebulous term, since it conveys urgency but does not define an acceptable time limit, and therefore relies on the sense of responsibility, priority and urgency of the person performing the action.*

Action - *if you allocate responsibility for an action to more than one person, it is likely that no-one will lead it, so each action must be attributed to only one member of the management team, although it can be done through a member of their department (for example, TD >RM means that TD is responsible for ensuring that RM does it, but TD nevertheless retains full responsibility for completion of the action).*

Management cycle - *note that items raised in the weekly performance report (SA2-A) issued on the previous day are considered before the meeting and actions instructed, otherwise there would be little point in issuing the weekly report.*

Narrative style - *just do it.*

Next meetings - *to develop the management team, Demo Company has each team member chair the weekly meetings in rotation, and it is essential that they all have the meetings in their diaries well in advance (monthly meetings should preferably be fixed a year in advance) - note that the first meeting in November is a directors' meeting, to consider the October results in full, while they are still warm.*

Minute taking - *it is good practice for each team member to take minutes in rotation, but remember that the minute-taker will write them from his own point of view, and the chief executive of the company will want to ensure that the minutes are a complete and accurate record of the agreed actions - the author takes his own minutes of most management meetings in which he participates (even if one of the team is taking formal minutes), to keep track of the issues and control over the team.*

Distribution - *for weekly minutes, the minute-taker allocates an hour after the meeting in his diary to write, check and issue the minutes, so that the management team has them within two hours of the meeting (DB in Taiwan, eight hours ahead, will pick them up on his e-mail and issue the necessary instructions to his team by e-mail or telephone) - less frequent (e.g. monthly) minutes should be issued within one working day of the end of the meeting.*

The Report Report
Notes and Observations

Demo Company Limited
MINUTE of meeting of MANAGEMENT - 0800, TUE 14 OCT 200X

Present: **Helga Riemann** / Don Chetham / Phil Jupp / Tanya Dobrolubov
Apologies: Duane Bradley (in Taiwan)

1	**Financial performance**		**Date**	**Action**
Orders	High intake needed wks 3/4/5 - ensure sales team pursuing		immed	DB
Staff	No workload complaints so far after reorganisation - be alert		ongoing	All
O/H	Essential overhead only until cumulative profit back on budget		ongoing	All
Kappa	Margin appears low - confirm current design spec		15-Oct-0X	TD > KM
C of S	Provide updated schedule of costs per product		17-Oct-0X	HR
Sales	Provide updated schedule of allowable sales prices & discounts		17-Oct-0X	HR

2	**Marketing & sales**		**Date**	**Action**
Exhibs	All sites booked up to end Jun 0Y			
	Book half-size stand for Infomex Aug 0Z		15-Oct-0X	DB > LJ
	Agree grant position with export development agency		immed	HR
Kappa	Feedback from distributors good, except for stabiliser problems			
	Set up marketing for launch at ExoTek in Jan 0Y		22-Nov-0X	DB > LJ
Web	Update website for exhib schedule and Kappa launch		22-Nov-0X	DC
	Instruct Dromedary to remedy link-rot problem - no extra fee		17-Oct-0X	DC
Distribs	Meet AustroMex and issue ultimatum - no price concessions		31-Oct-0X	DB
	Ensure Klagens available to step in if Austromex default		24-Oct-0X	DB
Team	Customer calls misrouted - ensure LJ & TA on standby rota		immed	DB
	Put HF & IP on exporters course		24-Oct-0X	DB

3	**Operations**		**Date**	**Action**
Supply	No major shortages - surplus of TX cases depleting slowly			
	Finalise 12 mth contract with Harrison Rule		20-Nov-0X	PJ
Stock	Convert extra TX motherboards to TC2 and dispose of		16-Nov-0X	PJ > AF
	Demo stock now under marketing - reduce & maintain < £240K		16-Oct-0X	PJ > DB
Prodn	Train 3 more staff on board assembly		21-Nov-0X	DB > JE
Plant	Heat treatment unreliable - repair before Kappa starts		ASAP	DC
Factory	Sprinkler system inspection due - check beforehand		23-Oct-0X	DC

4	**Research & development**		**Date**	**Action**
Kappa	Standardise on Laforga stabiliser and give BOM to finance		31-Oct-0X	TD > team
	Transfer product to production		28-Nov-0X	TD > DC
Epsilon	Chase up spec from Berlin - threaten cancellation		ASAP	DB
Dept	Present quarterly development plan to management		07-Nov-0X	TD > team
	Ensure all undocumented s/w fully documented by version no		28-Nov-0X	TD > RM

4	**Other**		**Date**	**Action**
Capex	Obtain additional system server on operating lease £4,277		24-Oct-0X	HR
Staff	Gill Railson to start in Inventory Control - arrange induction		03-Nov-0X	PJ
Legal	Confirm status of delay clause in SSP Orient contract		20-Oct-0X	DB

Next meetings - chair					
	Don Chetham	08.00	Tuesday	21-Oct-0X	Mgt team
	Phil Jupp	08.00	Tuesday	28-Oct-0X	Mgt team
	Duane Bradley	10.30	Tuesday	04-Nov-0X	**Directors**
	Tanya Dobrolubov	08.00	Tuesday	11-Nov-0X	Mgt team

The Report Report
Notes and Observations

THE REPORT REPORT - INDEX

THE REPORT REPORT - INDEX

THE REPORT REPORT - INDEX

THE REPORT REPORT - INDEX

THE REPORT REPORT - INDEX